Hilarious! Insane! Brutally honest! *Confessions Of An Ironman* was all of these things and more. Truly a delight to read.
Orad Elkayam | Founder, MoGi Group

What I appreciated most about *Confessions Of An Ironman* was that David Solyomi didn't begin as a top level competitor. In every aspect, he was your average Joe. Yet, that is the thing that makes his story even more inspiring! This incredible story shows the true power of self-determination.
Aaron Vick | CEO, Cicayda; Chief Visionary Officer, TCDI

There were only two things that I was thinking while reading *Confessions Of An Ironman*: this guy is certifiably crazy, and I would love to grab a beer with him! David Solyomi did a fantastic job of portraying the numerous highs, lows, and emotional turning points of his fight for the title Ironman. It was an inspiration just to live the experience vicariously. Moreover, Solyomi spices his work with numerous anecdotes pertaining to characters who have influenced his life going all the way back to his childhood. They act as markers as he travels his path to financial independence.
Eric Wentz | bestselling author of Zero Two Hundred Hours

David Solyomi has written an incredible memoir about the trials and tribulations one faces when they definitively make up their mind to test the limits of their spirit. A moving and highly enjoyable book!
Steve Ferreira | CEO, Ocean Audit Inc.

Confessions Of An Ironman was both funny and raw at the same time. What I loved is that Solyomi isn't afraid to laugh at himself and some of the ridiculous situations he gets himself into. At the same time, however, there's always an undertone of more serious wisdom and it's this combination that makes this book a winner in my opinion.

Levantay Vanessa OConnor | CEO, Levantay Enterprise LLC & USA Today bestselling author

What this man put himself through in the name of a dream...it's truly miraculous. *Confessions Of An Ironman* was as enjoyable as it was humbling to read. It just goes to show you, we are capable of so much more than we think!

Ray Brehm | CEO, TheSummitGuy.com

I cannot recommend this book enough! If you're looking for an interesting read that gets you fired up and ready to execute – *Confessions Of An Ironman* has it all!

Joseph LaPorta | CEO/Board Director/Author, Healthcare Linens Services Group

David Solyomi embodies the radical notion that anyone, anywhere, can get out there and accomplish their dreams if they simply refuse to give up or be swayed by negative circumstances. In that regard, *Confessions Of An Ironman* was a fantastically motivating literary experience!

Arif Anis | Founder & CEO of Global Clout

I can't say this book has made me want to attempt an Ironman myself, but it certainly has fired me up to go out there and get after a few of my own dream list items. David Solyomi has just the right touch of humor and inspiration, without ever coming across as preachy or condescending. He's just a man with a plan that refused to give up – and that's worth celebrating!

Michael Middleton | Founder, Pro-Vision Lifestyles

Not for the faint of heart! *Confessions Of An Ironman* was a grueling journey to peak physical fitness. The author does a wonderful job, however, at taking a subject that could have been monotonous and imbuing it with life, character, and charisma. A great addition to my library!

Robert Ellis | Owner, Ellis Editorial

Captivating! David Solyomi does an incredible job of putting you in the thick of the experience so that his triumphs – and disasters – feel as real and personal as if they were happening to you!

JenJen | Creator, Cool Jellybeans!

CONFESSIONS OF AN IRONMAN

SWIM, BIKE, AND RUN TO SELF-DISCOVERY

David Solyomi

Copyright © 2021 David Solyomi
Published in the United States by Leaders Press.
www.leaderspress.com

All rights reserved. No part of this book may be reproduced or transmitted in any form or by any means, electronic or mechanical, including photocopying, recording, or by an information storage and retrieval system – except by a reviewer who may quote brief passages in a review to be printed in a magazine or newspaper – without permission in writing from the publisher.

ISBN 978-1-63735-107-9 (pbk)
ISBN 978-1-63735-108-6 (ebook)

Print Book Distributed by Simon & Schuster
1230 Avenue of the Americas
New York, NY 10020

Library of Congress Control Number: 2021909766

"If you want the great things
life has to offer, you need to read
Confessions of an Ironman."

Allan Pease
Author of eleven #1 Bestsellers
Times #1 best-selling author

July 30, 2016

I had only slept an hour and a half. It turned out that the final lesson the Ironman had in store for me remained for the night before the race. My own destructive thoughts kept me awake. "You are still afraid of the water! What will happen to you in a 100-feet deep lake with 700 real athletes kicking you around?" There were moments when I found myself out of my body, watching my own struggle; I was the main actor in my own drama, fully identifying with the role. "I have to complete the race within 12 hours. With this much preparation, that is the minimum. At least that's what they are all saying; that is what I have been told. I am sure my teammates will all do it...but what about me?"

A vivid flashback from my childhood included the careless words of my mother. "If you quit karate, you'll amount to nothing and simply become a small-time nerd lawyer." I did quit karate when I was 13. Now, 21 years later, only a few hours stand between me and the start of an Ironman. "Am I doing this to prove something? If so, to whom, and why?"

My heart was thumping so hard that any chance of sleep was completely gone. My nervousness subsided for short periods of time when I realized that I did not have to compare myself to anyone, and it did not matter what the others were going to do. I only needed to focus on myself. Based on my preparation, there was no question that I could complete the race. Despite a few moments of calm, my time goal and the continuous comparison of my performance with that of others kept an overwhelming pressure hovering over me.

Since my half Ironman race, I have put in eight and a half months of systematically planned preparation and managed to put roughly 500 training hours under my belt. The work has been done. I am good enough to complete an Ironman. "But when will I be good enough for myself? When will I allow myself to enjoy what I have been working for?" Everything is decided in one's head and I still have a few hours to get things straight upstairs.

And then – just like the bell that saves the boxer after a round more difficult than planned – my 4 a.m. alarm signaled that the lesson was over, the teaching had been done, and it was solely up to me to make use of the realizations learned during the night. The alarm also signaled the beginning of a brand-new act; the actor in the main role had a job to do since the Ironman was not going to complete itself.

I didn't even know what an Ironman was when I decided I must become one. The ever-so-knowledgeable Google shed light on its definition and made it clear that in order to earn such a title I needed to complete a triathlon. At the time, I could barely swim, I had last sat on a bike when I was in my teens, and as for running... well, actually, I could run pretty well – for the better part of about half an hour. But it was too late to ponder all that now. I was saved by the "bell." I realized that it saved me from my own thoughts, but who would save me in a few hours' time when it would all be over and it would be declared, "Dávid Sólyomi, you are an Ironman"? And make no mistake, it would be declared, that is for sure. I have no plan B. I never have had one and all I've ever achieved has been approached that way. When it's all over, I will have a whole lot of time on my hands to face all the things I've learned instead of hiding from them behind the challenge ahead.

For now, though, I have to put all that aside and come back to it later. The longest day has arrived and I have a job to do.

Thirty-nine times. That is how often Anikó's name comes up in this book. She deserves much more credit as she was the woman who stood by me through it all, even before the insane Ironman decision and she was the one who accompanied me through the whole journey described herein. She supported me wholeheartedly with tolerance second to none. If not for her, I would not be the man I am today – the man I became on this journey. I am grateful that we were together over the course of these adventures.

CONTENTS

The Buried Manuscript 17

I. On Shaky Foundations

How It All Started 22

A Blank Canvas 27

    The Birth of the Three-step Goal Realization Recipe 28

The Starting Point (The "Caveman Portrait" of an Aspiring Ironman) .. 32

Over 3 Miles in Open Water Sounds Challenging Enough! 36

Headfirst into the Wall 40

"A Marathon? Get Real! There Is No Way You Can Do That" 44

The *Game* Which Changed It All 47

The Nutrition Plan? I Packed a Carrot Which, Unfortunately,
Froze Stiff in My Pocket 51

Life Will Never Be the Same 53

A Medal Would Be Nice! 56

II. Alone Against the World

A Dream or a Goal? 64

What a Pretty Medal! Have You Been to Rome? 75

This Bike Was Waiting for Me! 79

I Picked Out the Ideal First "Race" 81

    Caught by the Guard Rail 83

    From the Swimming Pool to the Hospital 83

There Goes My Triathlon Virginity, the Night After a Wedding 88

Sights on the Medal that Says Ironman 93

13

Confessions of an Ironman

If That Is How One Should Ride a Bike,
Then I Don't Know What I'm Doing!.................................. 100

Race Week at the Peak of Exhaustion................................. 101

The Morning Has Come! "Are You Going to
Wear That Blanket for the Swim?" 104

Ironman 70.3 Budapest: A Series of Surprises............................ 106

Is This It? Or Is This Only Half the Journey? I'll Run This Home
Court Marathon, and Then I'll Think It Over 112

Me? To the Podium? Are You Sure? 115

Two Days, Two Talks, and a Decision Taking Shape 119

This is Not Going to Work! I Need Help! 125

Keep Moving Attitude... 136

Mistakes Through the Eyes of an Expert: I Went Down the List
and Didn't Miss One.. 139

III. On a Controlled Path

A New Era and Many Surprises 144

A Parallel Project 150

Without Eating or Sleeping... 152

In Case I Got Used to It 157

It Feels Like It Is Time for a Marathon 164

The Second Shock 167

It Was Not an April Fool's Day Joke, Unfortunately 170

It Started out as a Reward Marathon 172

I Had Been Avoiding Group Rides..................................... 174

There Will Never Be a Better Chance to Give Up!....................... 179

What Does the Ironman Preparation Demand from a Rookie? 188

Hibernated Life and Derailed Dress Rehearsals......................... 190

A Weekend Program? I'm All Set, Thank You 193

"You Do a Half Ironman just for Training?" 199

Contents

Let's See the Course! 205

We Outgrew the Country 209

I Knew It Was Well Within My Reach, and I Immediately
Wanted More! 214

    Before the Race, Over the Peak 217

The Longest Day 222

What About the Paper? 236

Why Did I Do It After All? 241

What Now? The Role of Sports in My Life 244

IV. Bonus Round

Ironman Barcelona, Here I Come! 250

Contrast: The Night Before the Race 253

The Second "Longest Day" 255

Now I Can Let Go 260

No Excuses! 261

Appendix

The Training Plan for the 2016 Nagyatád Race 269

The Training Plan for the 2018 Ironman Barcelona 271

THE BURIED MANUSCRIPT

The preparation for my very first Ironman did not start at a level ground zero. Both mentally and physically, I started from a point lower than that. Professional athletes keep a training log. I, on the other hand, kept a record of my thoughts through my years of preparation. I had no idea whether I was going to actually reach my goal – the red carpet of the Ironman – which, at the time, seemed totally unattainable for me. In spite of that, I still felt a very strong urge, time and again, to write about the things I came to realize during my practice sessions, or in any other extreme situation I stumbled upon on the road – and let me tell you, as you will soon find out, extreme or even comic situations were not sparse on this journey.

Following the completion of my first Ironman, this diary-like manuscript laid untouched for two years as I was unsure whether I should turn it into a book. The shift in my indecision came one evening at a friendly get together where a girl I trained with in our triathlon club spoke to me about such profound feelings connected to her Ironman dream, a dream she has not yet realized, that it got me thinking: perhaps what I had to say about my own journey might speak to her as well. I put off sending her the manuscript for weeks because I clearly remembered, even though two years had passed, that my writing was not even close to a collection of various pieces of professional advice written to help a first-timer attempting the

Ironman. Rather, it was about an emotional journey of an ordinary human being, including some details which, in hindsight, I must say I was not really proud of. Eventually, I did hit the send button. Reni gave me the final push to make the manuscript into a book because, as she later explained, she got so immersed in it at times that she occasionally got lost in Budapest on the public transport while reading it. When she told me that my lines often brought tears to her eyes, and in the next moment some of my stories also made her laugh, I decided that if others could get a fraction of what my hidden pages had given her, I would gladly disclose them to the public.

What you are holding in your hands is by no means an Ironman training handbook. It has not even been written by a professional triathlete. I have completed only two long-distance triathlons so far; the first one in 11 hours and 33 minutes and the second one in 10 hours and 49 minutes. Neither of these times would make me competitive in the professional field nor do they empower me to give expert advice in triathlon training. I am not knowledgeable in this field which is why I asked for professional help in the later part of my preparation. (Had I gone to someone for help earlier, my book would be short a good number of comic stories.) You will not read about the optimal pedal cadence nor will you receive information about the ideal nutritional plan in the pages to follow. Nevertheless, I am willing to risk that, regardless of what you may expect, you are in for a surprise. The Ironman preparation gives the skeleton of the story and I did my best, wherever possible, to detail the discoveries and thoughts that emerged during my journey of self-discovery.

You may see this adventure of self-discovery wrapped in a sport costume as an entertaining read, but if you are brave enough to dig deeper, you could find numerous personally relevant and sometimes quite uncomfortable questions on the pages to follow. In the right hands, this book can become a harsh but honest mirror, and I am certain that looking into that mirror is immeasurably harder than participating in any Ironman race. Or perhaps that is the very thing that makes the Ironman so difficult (for a hobbyist like myself): before crossing the finish line, first you must face yourself.

The Buried Manuscript

Ádám Diószegi, a yoga instructor, said, "The best way to decide whether a man has truly looked inside himself about a given situation is to see if he eventually discovers something he is not quite happy about." I have discovered much as I have walked the path lain down by the Ironman, and since I did not flee from the challenges, a I aspects of my life have changed. What you gain from the pages which follow is entirely up to you.

I. ON SHAKY FOUNDATIONS

HOW IT ALL STARTED

It was lunchtime at the office on August 23, 2012, and I was sitting at my desk chatting with a friend. I credit Gmail Chat and not my flawless memory with the accuracy of the date. The conversation went something like this: *(I am saying "something like this" because I have decided to omit some of the actual words we used.)*

me:	this Ironman thing sounds very tough – I'd need at least a year if not more to
	prepare for it – in my condition that is
Laci:	yeah, and a bike too... :)
me:	it would be quite a challenge using my mom's old two-wheeler *but* that would get
	me on TV, I bet.
	the chain is kinda' loose on it too
Laci:	why not go *all* out if going for it
me:	at least it's got a light – I'd be going until it was dark, I guess
Laci:	sure, yeah...
	good thinking
me:	they'll flock to see that, I am sure
	hey, they may even sell tickets just for that
	the thing is that I don't know which year to set in sight that's realistic though
	2013 seems a bit early

Laci:	no way!
	that's exactly what should make it a *hit*
	do you know who won the 100 meter freestyle in the last Olympics...?
	...but I am sure most can immediately recall Erik the Eel – everyone will remember that guy for sure!
me:	wait, wait...it says a few things here I have not even thought of:
	"Don't leave checking your lists to the last day before leaving, because finding out you have a flat or realizing you forgot the Vaseline for the wetsuit could..."
Laci:	Vaseline?
	what's going on at these races anyway?
me:	yeah, what's that...?
	I think I should go see one first...
	you've done some biking before
	that 112-mile ride is pretty f....ing long all at once, isn't it?
Laci:	it is a whole f...ing lot
	my daily max has never been more than about 90 miles
	but in a whole day..., not in one go, for sure
me:	...I kinda thought so...
	and you cannot even bargain with them on the distances :)
Laci:	these dudes are full-on crazy
me:	well, I think I'm gonna let this idea soak some more

Confessions of an Ironman

There were so many things that needed soaking, but most importantly, I should have given myself more time. I was co-founder and director of a successful business venture, but still, I felt horrible those days. More and more decisions were being made in the company that I did not agree with, yet I did nothing to stand up for myself and, as a result, my self-esteem was plummeting. (*I was 30 then*.) That was my emotional state when I stumbled upon the idea of doing the Ironman. From an outside vantage point, my underlying motivation may be very clear. I needed a nice, long journey to break out of the cage I had built for myself.

I completed my first long-distance triathlon on July 30, 2016, and did not even think about a second one at that time. In the course of the four years that followed the little chat above, my life had completely changed. I read hundreds of books, participated in numerous seminars both locally and abroad, I achieved complete financial independence as an investor, left the operative board of the company I co-founded, and through an internet portal which started as a mere hobby, and with the release of my first book, was able to touch the lives of thousands of people. During that time I was also making steady progress in my sport activity, and in November, 2014 (more than two years after the chat I shared with you), I made the decision from which nothing and no one could deter me: "I will complete an Ironman, even if it is the last thing I ever do."

The Ironman preparation described herein provides a framework for sharing the learnings that brought change into my life. I felt many times during my preparation that the life principles taught by world-famous and highly expensive coaches, and which I had already been able to test and apply by then, are clearly reflected in sport. The "recipe for success" is similar almost anywhere you look. The Ironman went further than simply teaching me lessons, though; it gave me much more. It took me to extremes during training which enabled me, even if only for split seconds at a time, to view myself from the outside. In those mental states I was able to see things with exceptional clarity. The nature of the realizations were so unique that I felt it would have been a sin not to write them down.

When I started this adventure, I wasn't prepared for a great many things. What I mean isn't limited to my physical condition; in that regard, I wasn't even near the vicinity of the shape I needed to be in, as you'll soon find out. What caught me by greater surprise was what I learned about myself and about those closest to me during the toughest months of my preparation. I never thought that my Ironman project would have such a profound effect on the people around me, they acted as a "mirror" – in many cases without their knowledge – which would lead me to invaluable learnings. When talking about these experiences I will do my best not to offend anyone, but my priority here is to share the whole truth. I don't want to lose any of it by simply trying to remain polite.

Tony Robbins, the world's number one peak performance coach, taught me once in London that the majority of people are driven by two basic fears. One of these is that "*I am not good enough*" and the other, resulting directly from the previous one, is that "*I will not be loved.*" If you look around, you may find that so many people are caught up in trying to reach something they feel would catch others' attention, something they could be recognized for, even if it is only for a moment, and hence receive some sort of validation that they are good enough and likeable. (Think about it – what makes social media so successful? It is no doubt an ingenious business model to provide a platform, a place where the messages of those with unquenchable thirst for validation can appear in a nicely groomed form.) Could these two predominant fears have anything to do with the fact that participation in marathon and Ironman races is growing at an unprecedented rate all over the world? It is not even necessary to highlight any one special event because no matter which one I looked at, the trend was unmistakable.

There was a scene in *Cool Runnings*, a film about the Jamaican bobsled team, where the coach turns to his worried athletes and says, "A gold medal is a wonderful thing. But if you're not enough

Confessions of an Ironman

without it, you'll never be enough with it." The Ironman will not make anyone "good enough," but it does have the potential – like any road that leads to something seemingly impossible at first glance – to help you learn all you need to feel good about yourself, to lead a life that you enjoy. It is clear to me today that I was already a unique and good person before I set my mind to completing the Ironman. When I began my journey, however, I was light-years away from the state of consciousness that this journey helped me reach, along with so many similarly important truths which now are fundamental in how I live my life. To me, a true Ironman is someone who attains a mature and balanced mental state by the time he or she reaches the finish line. The physical aspect of the *story* is merely the tip of the iceberg...

A BLANK CANVAS

I wasn't completely satisfied with my life when I was around 29-30 years old, but I also knew if I wanted change, there was only one person who could do something about it. One of my first and best decisions was to commit to reading at least one hour every day. I wanted to learn, so I was willing to get out of bed at 5:30 a.m. every weekday. I predominantly read self-improvement and investing-related books.

I recognized the fact that change and progress could only be realized by stepping out of one's comfort zone. Consequently, no matter how unpleasant it was, I forcefully put myself into situations outside of my usual and comfortable patterns. I consciously and systematically sought out such events and that is how I found myself at a four-day course entitled *Drawing on the Right Side of the Brain* in October 2012.

I was the only participant not interested in drawing, not to mention my *refined* manual dexterity – let me just say that in elementary school, when trying to write, I punched holes in the paper for a long time. It was highly doubtful that I could actually draw something and, as a result, I was quite certain that I had found a place where I would be able to gain invaluable experience.

Confessions of an Ironman

THE BIRTH OF THE THREE-STEP GOAL REALIZATION RECIPE

On the first day, I drew a caveman-looking creature. This would have been just fine had the task not been a self-portrait. "No big deal," I thought, and was actually quite amused by my work until I got a chance to see what the others had drawn. Everyone was good – at least compared to me. I realized I was surrounded by all kinds of artistic people with very similar interests, while I, the rational economist, company director, and investor, was there *merely* to seek realizations about myself without the slightest intention of wanting to learn how to draw.

My "caveman" from the first day.

This was the mindset I started with and the drawing course turned out to be one of the most valuable investments I have ever made. The *self-portrait* we were asked to draw on the first day was simply a starting point and meant to be used as a basis of comparison to our last day's work. The learning began. We used tools which I had never imagined associated with drawing – sandpaper, Kleenex, and other similarly weird stuff. After a few exercises using these *tools*, I began to see why we were asked to work with them and how they could be applied to doodle around on the paper so that (as in the case of all the other participants) the outcome would look convincing. There were other tasks where we had to physically measure this-and-that and, as a result, we had to develop a larger "project" (the art teacher didn't call it that, I am sure) in smaller segments, putting it together slowly, step by step.

What I first had to realize was that I was shamefully impatient. Soft and soothing music played, which was meant to stimulate our right-side brain functioning, but it got on my nerves (in the beginning). I got so agitated that by the second day, if I recall correctly, I even went to lunch by myself, although Anikó, my girlfriend, was also there participating in the course. I could not put up with anyone including myself. I had a lot to think about at the end of each day as this experience certainly put me out of my comfort zone.

On the fourth day, we received our final task: We were given a large sheet of paper and were *simply* asked to draw a self-portrait based on a photograph. "When you're finished, you can go home," she said. That last sentence got me going...and here is what I managed to put together:

A few days later.

Confessions of an Ironman

Now, I am quite certain they will not start using my work to advertise this course in the future, but the transformation that jumped out at me from the paper compared to what I had created only a few days before was astonishing to me. My impatience took over once again and I tried to convince the teacher that I had achieved what I had come for. Even though she still saw things here and there that could have been improved upon, I suspect she realized, after listening to my speech, that any further attempt on her part to convince me to keep working would have been in vain so we said our goodbyes.

The drawings never made it further than my storage room, but the three-step goal realization recipe I discovered while working on them has stayed with me ever since and I use it in all aspects of my life. Here are the steps I had to go through to reach a goal which seemed completely unattainable at first, the drawing of a terrifyingly large (A3-size – 11.0 x 17.0 in) self-portrait:

1. I had to get familiar with some of the techniques which are usually effective in doing a project like that. (Sandpaper, paper, tissue… I'd rather leave the list incomplete so that I don't have to *relive* the entire experience.)

2. I had to divide the task into smaller segments. After receiving the blank A3-sized paper, we had to identify a number of critical spots in proportion to our photograph, we had to measure them out, thus making the project seem more doable as it got split into smaller subparts. *(The Ironman is no different in that regard – even the professionals say they don't think of it as one whole.)*

3. Finally, my favorite part of the recipe, we had to start the work and keep at it until it was done. As Tony Robbins likes to say, *"Take massive action!"*

A Blank Canvas

Theoretical knowledge is nice and all, but eventually you must get down to it and do the work. Any excuses or plan Bs are ruled out. Ultimately, I learned how to realize a goal: I researched the details, then divided the task into smaller chunks, making each of them attainable mini-goals. After that, there was nothing else left to do other than to actually take the first step on the road to completion, focusing on only one piece of the puzzle at any given moment.

The drawing course was an ideal place for learning and the construction of the recipe. In that artificial environment it was very easy to isolate the individual steps needed for success. In real life, on the other hand, I set many goals where I had to re-evaluate my position and return to step one so that I could learn more and acquire additional information, even though I was already in the final phase of execution. This three-step approach has always worked for me; the ability to take a step back when working on a large project and identify which phase I'm in, what I am doing, and why, has always proven to be constructive. I could not have completed the Ironman any other way.

THE STARTING POINT (THE "CAVEMAN PORTRAIT" OF AN ASPIRING IRONMAN)

I need to tell you about the foundation on which I so boldly based my Ironman adventure to provide more perspective about what you're about to read. In light of my base state, the idea was more like the insane undertaking of a troubled mind than a well-calculated and thought-out plan.

Swim: My mom doesn't get near water that is not shallow enough for her to walk in. My dad, although not out of his element in a pool, wouldn't be offended if I said he is not even close to being a proper swimmer. As a child, I followed mom's model and, as a direct result, was utterly terrified every single year when – as part of the compulsory physical education program in school – they wanted to teach me how to swim. Stepping into my teens, it started to get really uncomfortable to constantly feel that I would rather hide during those nightmare PE lessons, counting the seconds until the end, while all the others were having a blast swimming. Not to mention that this macho act of mine must have gone over *really well* with the girls, too. Right around then I actually started to care about that and this handicap was beginning to bother me beyond belief. Nevertheless, no matter how humiliating it was, it still didn't give my swimming career a jump start.

The breakthrough came at a family vacation. I decided to slip out of my parents' sight, get into a pool by myself, and was crazy enough to make peace with the thought that if things went south, the worst-case scenario was that I would drown. I don't recall what exactly inspired my impulse, but I do remember that in my preadolescent despair, I went for it with a life-sucks-anyway attitude. The result was astonishing! I sank, but a few moments later I was back at the surface. I had been told many times before that this would happen, but I was always so frightened that I never actually held out until that point and went into panic mode much sooner instead. After I had the floating experience under my belt, all I needed to do was simply add the strokes I had been taught all those years before – which I never really thought I would ever make use of. For the very first time in my life, I was actually swimming.

When I told my mom about my revelation, I got to experience yet another *first* – I got the biggest slap I had ever received up until then, and ever since, for that matter. Apparently, she was not very happy that I left her side without saying a word, and the fact that the whole place ended up looking for me did not make the situation any better. So, instead of reassurance and encouragement, her version of a response was a bit different.

Eventually, I learned the breaststroke and later, in the summer months of my high school years, I regularly got up at 6 a.m. and rode my bike to the local pool to swim 1500 meters. Following these sessions, like any decent high school student, I went right back home and slept until noon. This sums up my background in swimming which, in actuality, was my strongest discipline out of the three.

Bike: I had one – eventually. But I can see how anyone could take me for an oddball if I told them when all my friends had long been enjoying spinning around our block, I still didn't know how to ride a bike. Does this make me weird? Maybe. As embarrassing as this may sound, I willingly admit it. I was well into my elementary school years when my grandfather taught me how to ride, and when I managed to convince my grandma that it was dire that I had a mountain bike, since practically everyone had one. When I got it, I didn't use it anywhere but in the small town I lived in at the time. I

Confessions of an Ironman

am sure it does not come as a surprise that my bike handling skills were not the best either. I almost got hit a couple of times, so I ended up only getting on that thing when absolutely necessary to move around in town.

The only time I broke this routine, in hopes of getting an "A" in PE, was when I signed up for a bike tour which took me off road and onto some dirt paths around town. I practically wept by the time I reached the finish. Either my brakes were in fact touching the rims the whole time and that is why I was so slow, or perhaps my report of this mishap was so convincing, that by now I don't remember whether it was really true. The point is that I had no business being on a bike whatsoever and neither did I want to have anything more to do with it.

Run: From ages 10 to 13, I did karate and we had to run 2.5-5 miles every week. The problem was that once I moved to Budapest to attend college, my lifestyle was not exactly exercise-focused, to say the least. After karate, my next running-related experience, which happened in my twenties, was when I managed to convince Anikó to check out a track in Budapest. Naturally, I thought I'd do the *usual* five miles since that's what I had been used to running in my earlier days. Without going into any painful details, I'd just like to say that I did not manage to run five miles – I hardly did half of that. After realizing how disastrous a shape I was in, though, I decided to go back and run a little every week. I ended up going once or twice a week and ran about four miles at around an 8-minute per mile pace, which I thought was just fine.

In light of my background I think it is understandable, even though the intent to become an Ironman was within me, that I was afraid to make it a defined goal. Slowly, step by step, I wanted to assess whether it was realistic that I could actually reach that level someday.

Google made it clear that this project meant a 2.4-mile swim, a 112-mile bike ride, and a marathon, which is a 26.2-mile run. The entire project was just as terrifying as the blank, A3-sized paper at the

The Starting Point (The "Caveman Portrait" of an Aspiring Ironman)

drawing course; it had to be divided up into smaller segments. I did not own a bike, the marathon seemed absolutely impossible, but I felt the 2.4-mile swim was not unattainable even though I had not been to a pool for years. Perhaps that is the very reason why I somehow believed completing the swim would not be out of reach. If we're talking a three- step recipe and division of tasks, why not start with this latter one – let's see if I can actually swim 2.4 miles in one go.

OVER 3 MILES IN OPEN WATER SOUNDS CHALLENGING ENOUGH!

This stunt was done in the summer of 2013. Since I had not seen a pool for a few years, I was not quite sure what I was up against when I decided to tackle the 5.2-kilometer (3.2 miles) lake crossing in Balaton, which happens to be the largest lake in Central Europe. My thinking was that I ought to be able to swim 1500 meters with no problem – I had done that numerous times before. After that, all I would have left to swim in open water was 3700 meters. Somehow, I had a feeling it would be a good idea to test this in a pool before I actually signed up for swimming across a sizable lake.

The next thing I remember is that I am home by myself, diligently vacuuming the floor. At first glance, there seems to be nothing wrong with that. What makes it suspicious is that vacuuming is *the* very last thing I would think of doing in my spare time. I was so afraid to go to the pool that I decided to start cleaning in an attempt to avoid it. I clearly remember the moment when I recognized my fear. There was only one thing to be done and that was exactly what I did – I put down the vacuum, put my gear in my backpack as quickly as possible, and I took off to the tram stop. I intentionally did not give myself time to think twice about it. Trapped on the tram, of course, I could not avoid doing my calculations over how I used to

Over 3 Miles in Open Water Sounds Challenging Enough!

swim 30 lengths in a 50-meter pool every morning and that I was now getting ready to cover 5200 meters – which was exactly...104 lengths. The sizable difference between the two numbers was daunting but I was already rolling and that meant no turning back.

My only recollection of the pool "dress-rehearsal" is that it lasted over two hours and I covered the entire distance in breaststroke. Nevertheless, I did not give up. I am the kind of person who starts something and doesn't stop until it is done, no matter the cost. This is sometimes an advantageous trait to have but it can also work against you. The math theorem was evidenced by physical verification – the distance of 104 lengths of the pool was indeed three and a half times the distance I used to cover.

Later, when I had an actual training program, my coach always talked about the importance of gradual increases in workload, and that shocking the body with unreasonably large quantities of exercise at one time could backfire. The immediate result of my test swim was that I literally could not get out of the pool as my arms did not have enough strength left to push me out. When I came to realize the severity of the situation, all I could do was try to act natural and pretend that everything was perfectly fine, and I was simply enjoying the water while watching the other swimmers and passersby. It goes without saying that, in my book, asking for help was out of the question. The real show began after I was finally able to get out of the water. My sorry attempts to take steps on the deck could have easily been a scene in a zombie movie as I was trying to make it to the locker room with blood running down both my legs. It turned out that wearing those fashionable water shorts to swim 5200 meters was not a good idea after all because they chafed every square inch of the skin they came in contact with. The effect, no doubt, was dramatic with the blood and all - too bad the ominous musical accompaniment was missing. (The lifeguard on duty that day had no idea that some years later I would return with an even more horrifying performance.) In the final scene of this little episode, I am desperately holding onto the rails at the door of the tram as I am trying to make it down those last couple of steps.

37

Confessions of an Ironman

My legs had completely tightened up while sitting down. Eventually, I managed to make it home.

Consequently, I was very happy to learn that the lake crossing was postponed due to unfavorable weather, which allowed me some extra time for recovery. Plus, I could squeeze in a shopping trip to buy a pair of proper trunks that would not skin me to the bone. Naturally, testing my new gear was out of the question. "I had already swum the distance, the next time around will be in the lake," I decided.

It is without exaggeration that I was terrified of this swimming adventure. A picture that was taken right before the start tells it all – my facial expression, as I turn around to wave to Anikó, could easily be mistaken for that of a prisoner about to be executed. I was out of place, to say the least. I don't think there are words to describe one's mental state when that person is afraid of the water, doesn't have the slightest sense of security, but still takes the plunge to cover 5200 meters in the open water of a huge lake. Besides the immense fear, I recall freezing my butt off in the water – my memories are of purple lips, shivering, and the perpetual voice in my head saying, "I will never do such a stupid thing ever again! Naturally, I will finish, now that I have started, and I am sure I will be very proud of myself once I reach the other side, but that is it. The Ironman is out of the question."

Little did I know that my "never again" idea was doomed before my swim ended. Anikó regretted not joining me for the big swim and, by the time I finished my 2 hour 22 minute adventure, she had already decided to enter a 3800-meter bay crossing in the same lake the following (!) weekend. The least I could do was accompany her. That is how I found myself back in the ice-cold water – or at least I felt it was that cold – of Lake Balaton, struggling to make the experience less humiliating by keeping the gap between me and my girlfriend as small as possible. Just like the previous time, this was also a horrible experience.

Over 3 Miles in Open Water Sounds Challenging Enough!

All that aside, at least I could say that I was capable of completing the swim distance of a full Ironman: 3800 meters. Believing I could tick that box, it was time to move on to the next challenge to find out if this triathlon idea would amount to anything at all. One thing was still certain: Setting the Ironman as a goal was very far out. (*We were still in 2013 after all.*)

HEADFIRST INTO THE WALL

Since I did not own a bike, it was obvious that testing my ability to run was next in line. As for the distance, naturally, I set my eyes on a full marathon. *(Although I already had a hunch "a slow increase in workload" approach would not be a bad idea, I did not ask for the help of a professional coach until later.)*

The lake crossing happened on July 20, 2013. Not wanting to waste time, I decided to enter the Budapest Marathon scheduled in October of that same year. To complete a marathon, one merely has to run. So, similar to my approach to the swim project, I was convinced that running 26.2 miles was no different than running 4 – which I had been previously quite used to. "It should be no problem at all," I thought. All in all, the swim hadn't been too bad. Clearly, time can do wonders to our memories.

Challenges Are Vital to Stay Alive

I have made peace with the fact that I cannot remain still – I always need something to do, and I relentlessly search for the next adventure or exciting project because I refuse to live a dull, uneventful life. It seems as though research also supports the suggestion that challenges are indeed essential for a prolonged life.

There was an experiment conducted at the University of California at Berkeley that raises some very intriguing questions.

Scientists artificially created the absolute perfect living conditions for an amoeba, setting the most ideal temperature and light conditions, optimizing all aspects of its environment and also providing it with plenty of nutrients, and began to observe the outcome. Basically, they provided that little lifeform with everything it could possibly need. Can you guess what happened to it? The amoeba died. It did not have to make any effort to acquire anything to sustain life as all conditions were provided for survival, and that ended up being the very thing that killed it. Consequently, challenges, risks, and adventures are essential for survival. (It has also been observed in humans that a completely inactive lifestyle which very often follows an active life going into retirement, the sudden loss of a life purpose, and an abruptly vanishing motivation are not quite helpful in maintaining one's health. Knowing this, it does not come as a surprise that those who live a fulfilling life, occupying themselves with activities that are meaningful for them, willingly and wholeheartedly tackling each day, end up living longer. A traditional retirement is a misguided goal, which I came to realize quite late.)

I would like to show you my very own plan, precisely as it was conjured, which was intended to get me ready for a full marathon. In hindsight, knowing what I know now, I am fully aware how pitiful it is to put something like this down on paper.

Without further ado, here is the original plan in all its glory:

What do I have to do so that I can complete the Budapest Marathon on October 13, 2013?

1. In August I will run 9 miles (3 loops on Margaret Island)
2. In August I will run 12.5 miles (4 loops on Margaret Island)

Confessions of an Ironman

3. After my summer vacation, I will run 12.5 miles (4 loops on Margaret Island)

4. By the 20th of September, I will run 19 miles (6 loops on Margaret Island)

5. By the 1st of October, I will run 26 miles (8 loops on Margaret Island)

6. Following that, a few light 12-mile runs

7. On October 13th – Budapest Marathon

Typical of me, I found the beginning of the training plan a bit too light. According to my Nike application, I did my first Margaret Island run on August 3, 2013. I can recall very clearly that right around the 10K mark I was really proud of myself, thinking it was quite something already, and from that point on I was running in uncharted territory, as I had not done anything longer than 8K before. I felt pretty good so I thought, since I was out there already, why not go for a half-marathon, which I did in 1 hour and 56 minutes. Even though I had nothing to compare this experience to, I was convinced that the marathon should not be a problem at all if I was able to do what I had just done without practically any preparation. You must have noticed that I completely skipped the first step of my training plan. After all, why should one run only 9 miles if he is capable of more?!

In the next act, I went for 5 island loops which, following a 10-day (completely inactive) rest period, did not feel good at all. My knees, ankles, and basically every square inch of my body ached. No worries though. I thought to myself, "I have exceeded my plan and I am about to leave for a vacation from which I will return fully rested, hence the marathon shouldn't be a problem, for sure."

We went to Bali for two weeks, where I primarily practiced floating on water and consuming beer. Although I had my suspicions that this was not the optimal training regimen, I was quite convinced that I was tough enough and would make my plan work, no matter what – with no plan B, as always.

On September 15th, as a means to catch up with my plan, I ran 19 miles. I averaged a 10 minute mile pace and was completely spent. I was in all kinds of pain, and based on what my body was telling me, I was beginning to have serious doubts about the marathon. I kept postponing registering for the race. The 6 island loops were in the sack and, according to the plan, the next chunk was going to be 8 loops – the full distance, which, no matter what happened, I would have to get through regardless of how I felt.

It took one more week before I finally gave up my suicidal marathon project. The emotions that overtook me on that run are painfully vivid even now, as I had never been the type of guy who decides to quit. I managed to struggle through 6 island loops, but then there was nothing I could do; I simply could not continue. My knees and ankles had completely given out. I had lost a few toenails by then as well. To this day, I still do not know why Anikó had decided to throw her lot in with me in my insane project but she, too, ran that day. To say the least, she did not look any better than I by the end of the sixth lap. I was sitting on a bench when she came in and the only thing that stood between me and crying from the pain was whatever I had left of my pride; there were just too many people around to completely break down. As I recall, Anikó was relieved when I told her I had reached my limits and that was it, I had to let it go. We had parked far enough away that even the walk to the car inflicted excruciating pain, which burned the thought into my brain that "I am not so tough after all, at least not so much as to go at things so mindlessly."

I went back to my 4-mile runs and gave myself time to process what had happened. This marathon is out of reach, no question about it, and I have a full year before the next one. "The question is whether I should actually run it." I was certainly not ready to expose myself to such pain again, not to mention that I had no clue that the whole thing could, or rather, surely should be done differently.

"A MARATHON? GET REAL! THERE IS NO WAY YOU CAN DO THAT."

Inevitably, those nearest to me got word of my running debacle, which made me very uneasy since they, too, were under the impression I was the kind of person who did not give up easily. I was sure of myself in that respect as well; I always finished what I started! The pain caused by my foolishly hasty attempt was so ingrained that the marathon ended up occupying a spot, right next to the Ironman, on my list of goals I was too afraid to attempt. I seriously doubted that I was ever going to be able to complete one.

This doubt lasted until I heard something at the office. My partner and co-founder happened to tell me that the marathon was a distance that was surely beyond my limits. By then, we had had our fair share of conflicts. We had decided that I would be going to the office much less in the coming year, and that I would only work on my main projects. I needed no further motivation than this casual judgment which, I'm sure, was made without the slightest intent of malice. It could not have come at a better time or from a better person. My decision was made right at that moment: There will be no more failures. I will complete a marathon – and I won't wait until next October, the date of the following Budapest Marathon! *They say that a supportive environment can prove to be helpful.* Apparently, an unsupportive environment can sometimes work wonders as well.

"A Marathon? Get Real! There Is No Way You Can Do That."

I was back in the saddle and, without hesitation, I focused on an upcoming marathon being held the following March. After my first attempt, I recognized (*with overflowing wisdom*) that I was clueless as to how one should prepare for running such a distance. Nevertheless, I was certain my approach had to be completely different from my last attempt. I started reading up on the subject and what I found shocked me!

No matter how deep I dug, I could not find any sites, articles, or training plans on the internet which did not include at least four workouts per week. Four runs? Generally, it took me 2-3 weeks to run that many times. What's more, I came to realize that it was not a bad idea to mix in some shorter sessions instead of going all out every time and running as far as I could. Not to mention that the intensity could also be varied from time to time. The training recommendations were drastically different compared to the way I had been doing it, and I felt it would be best to first talk to some people I knew who had already run marathons. I reached out to a girl I knew on Facebook, who used to be a neighbor in my hometown of Jászberény, Hungary, and who, as I later learned, has actually earned a degree in Physical Education. She had completed the Oslo Marathon. Although, initially, she agreed to meet me over a coffee to discuss preparing for such a thing, she kept on finding excuses to postpone the meeting. Perhaps she thought that my marathon inquiry was simply a cover story so that I could meet up with her. Little did she know that I was only concerned with the marathon question at the time. That and the contemplation of how I could break free of my own company where I was not happy anymore, so that I could finally do something that I truly love, am passionate about, and through which I could create something of genuine value.

I gave up trying to persuade her to meet me, and not much later discovered a *"Coach"* menu item in the Nike running app I had been regularly using, where I could specify what I was preparing for and could enter the exact date of the event. I quickly set it up, designating the March marathon as my goal. I found myself staring

Confessions of an Ironman

at my phone at great length after the freshly generated beginner runners' (that would be me) marathon training plan appeared on the screen.

It was already nearing the end of December, so the first thing the app warned me about was that my preparation start was too late, which meant that I would need to pick up the work in an already higher intensity phase. Looking at the figures, though, I thought I could easily do what the plan prescribed in the first weeks, despite the fact that I would have to devote significantly more time to the running project than expected since the plan included a session almost every day. As for the weeks to follow, I was not concerned with them at that time. "I'll worry about that when I get there," I thought. I trusted the app – who was I to question it anyway? Whatever it asks for I will do, no questions asked. No plan B! Remember?

Arnold Schwarzenegger used to say that if you do not have a plan B, you have to make plan A work. If you are fully committed to something, the forces of the universe (or whatever one may call them) will stand behind you and support you. This has been proven to me several times.

THE GAME WHICH CHANGED IT ALL

The use of the mobile application brought consistency into my training with gradually increasing workloads. All I needed was disciplined execution, which I knew was one of my strengths. Each week I completed every session prescribed, granted, I did not pay attention to the instructions specifying the intensity (after all, I merely wanted to complete the distance). Besides ignoring this *small* detail, my other deviation was that I also combined some of the shorter runs so as to have more rest days, while still making sure that the weekly mileage requirements were met. In hindsight, I am fully aware that neither of these ideas were very clever but, somehow, I lucked out and managed to get it all done.

I followed the orders of the tyrant application. No matter what obstacle it put in my way, I was relentless. For instance, when I returned from my company's 2014 strategic planning weekend on a Sunday, completely exhausted and hungover, I still went out and did the work necessary to complete the weekly mileage. I frequently received peculiar remarks while running. On that particular weekend, for instance, an elderly man happened to tell me how envious he was of me, and how much he would have liked to be as young as I was and be able to run like that. I have a hunch he was drugged by my alcohol-filled perspiration.

Confessions of an Ironman

All in all, my sports endeavor was back on track. I had a plan, and that felt good. Unfortunately, this was the only aspect of my life at the time that I felt satisfied with. My company-related affairs made me so tense that my mood swings were steadily becoming intolerable. I started each day at 5:30 a.m., did yoga, meditated, and read before arriving at the office by 9:00 a.m., where my spirits were rapidly dragged back down from where I had managed to elevate them. The tension in me was enormous, and although I knew that it could not go on like that for much longer, I also could not see the way out.

Besides reading a lot, I also attended various programs aimed at self-improvement, which is how I ended up taking part in a satellite seminar in January, 2014, promoting Tony Robbins' Unleash the Power Within (UPW) London event. Interestingly enough, the seminar was on a day when I found myself in perhaps the deepest pit of my life up to that point – I was a mess. Obviously, finding myself at the seminar the same day was no coincidence. The program was well structured in all respects: I learned that Tony Robbins was the world's number one life coach who had helped a long line of famous and influential people among whom were presidents, star athletes, star investors, and basically a great many individuals coming from all walks of life. He also seemed like a nice guy. His videos were convincing and so was the fact that, although the cost of his one-on-one sessions reach the million-dollar mark, Tony also led seminars a few times a year, which were attended by thousands at a time and where many individuals had had profound breakthroughs in their lives. Oprah Winfrey, for instance, hailed him in a video following a fire walk experience. This was the sort of event the UPW was and it happened only once a year in Europe, in London. The price? I'd rather not talk about that – "Those are simply too many figures," I thought. Slightly disappointed, I accepted the facts, but then, as part of the program, I was asked to participate in a group game, in which all attending were supposed to take an active part. "Great," I thought. "This is all I need now." (Looking back, though, I can clearly see it was just what I needed, and it could not have come at a better time.)

The Game Which Changed It All

The game was very complex, based on a lot of interaction, and I could tell right away that winning it was no easy feat. The most significant thing I realized while playing was that after a few short minutes I could already see it would be impossible for me to win with the strategy I had chosen and the time was ticking away mercilessly. What did I do once this became clear to me? Nothing! I did absolutely nothing. I decided to give up and reverted to a *"let's just be done with it"* attitude, resigning completely. That is when the harsh blow hit me from the stage: "Have you been paying attention to your feelings and thoughts during the game? Wake up, because that is exactly the way you live your life! This game reveals it all!"

Wait a minute! This knocked the wind out of me. The message hit home. By then, I had been living a life without true fulfillment for so long that I completely lost sight of my own values. As time passed, they had gotten buried deep within me, and I was simply sitting back and waiting, *just to be done with it,* ruling out the possibility of victory entirely. But what is *it* that I just want to be done with? One more day? Another month? One more year? Life, as I know it! This confrontation at the age of 32 hit me with such force; the break following the "game" could not have come at a better time. Before they let us have a breather, though, we had to listen to the special offer for UPW London one more time.

As was usually the case, Anikó was with me at this event. My contemplations during the break reached their height in the restroom, so I'd rather spare you of the picture of what I was doing when pondering the following: "I'm completely and utterly f***ed up. I have to do something; I want to get myself up and out of this somehow. I need help. This Tony guy has a very impressive list of people he has been able to help. Too bad that this UPW is so brutally expensive. But now I am also in a position where I can actually afford to pay the fee and I really am in great need of some kind of change. Could there be a better time? If I wait and pass it up, later on, life will probably throw me a curveball again, but then I might not have the money. I am doing it! I am talking to Anikó, and we are signing up!"

49

Confessions of an Ironman

When I got back, Anikó and I blurted out, almost in unison, that we had to go to London. We made our decision; we paid the fee! I did not want to be playing the losing game of *let's-just-be-done-with-it* anymore and I was finally willing to do something about it. Let me tell you, having to pay a dollar sum well into the four-figure realm was way outside my comfort zone, but I also felt that, come March, something extraordinary was going to happen at the UPW in London, and my commitment would be greatly rewarded.

In March?! When I got home, I realized that the rendezvous with Tony was in *somewhat* of a conflict with my marathon race for which I was preparing so wholeheartedly, following every command of the pocket-tyrant mobile app day in and day out. I could not be in two places at the same time – there was no question about that, just like it was not a question whether I was running a marathon. As always, there was no plan B.

I had started my self-torture in December, and it was then the 25th of January. It was easy to accurately remember the date because, as part of a task at the seminar, we had written down where and what we saw ourselves doing in precisely five years' time. My paper has January 25, 2019, written on it. Still, to this day, I look at that note from time to time because the list I wrote in that state of mind is very interesting and, as a matter of fact, has items coming true one by one, even though they seemed so out of reach at the time.

I had already put about a month's work into my marathon preparation and my weekend runs were getting longer and longer. In a few weeks, I was going to start having over 19-mile runs on my plate; the idea became more and more daunting. I kept thinking that I should go ahead and round up one of these over-19-mile adventures a *bit* and put an end to the marathon dilemma; I could leave out the organized competition factor and just do it all on my own.

THE NUTRITION PLAN? I PACKED A CARROT WHICH, UNFORTUNATELY, FROZE STIFF IN MY POCKET

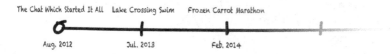

The big day fell on February 1, 2014. The thermometer showed 19 degrees Fahrenheit that morning and the Nike app asked for a 20-mile run. By then, the app and I had grown apart, to say the least. Although I had not defined it as an actual plan, I kept thinking that if I felt good enough, I would keep going and cover the whole 26.2-mile distance, then delete the app, forget about the non-stop training, and leave for London with the marathon project all done and dusted. I also considered the possibility that I could even get a bit hungry during the run, so I put a piece of carrot in the pocket of my windbreaker (since, at that point, I still did not own any proper training gear). My plan was that under no circumstances would I eat any of it until halfway through, since I was certain there was no need to take anything on board until after that point. As you can see, I was not quite up to speed on sports nutrition either.

Describing running a marathon would be like talking about the process of paint drying or how grass grows, so I will only share the more memorable moments. I was running along a creek in town when I was stopped by an old lady who asked if I knew of a good

Confessions of an Ironman

place to have a good slice of cake. It was 19 degrees! When I told her I was not a local and had no clue, she scoffed, waved her hand in disbelief, and told me not to kid her because she had seen me running there all the time! "One more reason to get this over with today," I thought.

I took the run easy so I felt well. About halfway through, I was ready for the carrot. When I bit into it, I almost broke my teeth. I did not consider the possibility that it would freeze stiff in the cold. At least it lasted longer that way. Around the 22-mile mark I had to take a short break because my cruel little mobile app, most likely sensing the end of our relationship, had killed my phone and it needed a quick charge. To my great disappointment, the application did not record the extra mile that it took me to run home. My phone was plugged in for about 5 minutes while I quickly took on board a small fruit shake (which proved to be a very bad idea), then I carried on to complete the assignment. I decided to finish up the last miles on a track nearby and I made sure to add on some extra mileage since I was certain that my iPhone would turn off at the moment I took it out to check the distance covered. It read 26.7 miles when I finally gathered the courage to look at it. It was loud and clear, right on the screen – I had completed the marathon distance in 4 hours and 24 minutes. My first reaction was very emotional, thinking I had finally done it, but then, instead of letting my tears out, I immediately started cursing Apple – at that very moment, my phone was completely depleted and went blank. I could not care less about the actual time taken, but as I was unable to do it in an organized event, I wanted a marathon completion recorded on at least one application. I am certain that not a lot of people do this alone, carrying a single piece of carrot, in winter, wearing a windbreaker, on the banks of a creek. Still, for me, it was the perfect way.

I had broken through another barrier! Nonetheless, I had no idea what should come next. I could not see past the London event in March, and I was filled with fear. I was going to have to step up to the plate once again, facing all kinds of challenges, including a fire walk.

LIFE WILL NEVER BE THE SAME

Tony Robbins' four-day event gave me more than I expected. We did the legendary fire walk the first evening, which gave proof to us all that given the proper preparation and the removal of barriers built in our heads, we are capable of doing the things we feared before. The energy of the crowd was indescribable and, in that environment, I was able to move past my strong reservations about excessive cheering and shouting, which I have never been able to appreciate before.

There was an exceptionally powerful exercise, called the Dickens Process, which was a guided visualization. Before we began, all children were escorted out of the room – we soon found out why. The more reserved ones in the crowd of 7000 just cried quietly, while others were screaming in agony. As I recall, we were asked to imagine a state of existence we longed for and then, as if we were living it, we had to soak in what it felt like. Then, Tony's instructions tore us drastically out of that idyll and focused our attention back to our current state, so that we could uncover all the negative things dragging us down. This exercise coupled the dreamed-up image with such deep desire while associating the situations preventing the dream from being realized with such excruciating pain, that it made it simply impossible for anyone to continue living their lives as they had done before. The chorus of the song "Life Will Never Be the Same" started to make a lot of sense, as it was played numerous times during the breaks.

Confessions of an Ironman

It is no coincidence that a great many people have profound breakthroughs at these events. Many, wasting no time, immediately start working on the problems they were previously afraid to face, which had been holding them back, possibly for many years. Clearly, for me, this problem was the role I played in my business venture. Even though, according to our agreement, I only had to go in twice a week and was doing all other work from home, it hardly changed the fact that I was doing something I did not want to do anymore. Not to mention that this halfway in, halfway out state was impossible to keep; it goes without saying which direction I would have liked it to shift. On top of it all, my relationship with my co-founder had also reached a painfully low point.

It was March, and I knew, no matter what decision I made, I would fulfill my existing agreements. This meant that I had to work until the end of September and I had to close two major projects. In the meantime, after the Dickens Process experience, there was no way I could just go home and carry on the way I had been and not change anything. I made an important decision: "I'm going to step out into the light, take the risk, and disclose what I am really interested in."

That is how osztalekportfolio.com (meaning dividend portfolio), my Hungarian website on dividend-focused stock investing, was born in May, 2014. I started it purely as a hobby, as a means of self-expression. By then, I had read a deluge of literature on the subject in English and a comprehensive system had formulated in my head. My approach made it possible to earn a steadily growing passive income in the form of dividends by buying partial ownership in publicly listed global companies. As a result, one could attain complete financial freedom. This was my childhood dream, and no matter how much money we made with our business, I never felt that I was getting closer to my goal until I gained the necessary knowledge, experience, and confidence in investing. (By the way, one of the world's most reputable investors, Guy Spier, also

Life Will Never Be the Same

highlights in his book that it was Tony Robbins' UPW that delivered a breakthrough in his life, too.[1])

I found myself feeling better just by doing something which I thought was worthwhile, convinced that it created real value. Even if only a handful of people found their way to my website initially, I still very much enjoyed writing there.

During an event session, Tony had asked if anyone had run a marathon. I proudly raised my hand and looked around to learn that there weren't too many of us among the 7000 participants. "Which of you could run a marathon right now?" Few hands stayed in the air. "And who thinks that they could run a marathon with the help of a professional coach?" It did not come as a surprise that many more hands flew high following that question. No matter what it may be, any goal can be realized – one simply has to learn the related techniques, divide the process up into smaller chunks, and then dive right in and start it. Sound familiar? My own recipe of success distilled from the drawing course stared right back at me, only wrapped differently coming from the world's number one peak performance coach. If at all possible, it is always a good idea to ask for professional help because it can speed up the process significantly. A though I did not yet have anyone to help me make my aspirations a reality, my life started to take more favorable turns after the UPW because I began to take massive action.

---

[1] Guy Spier is an investor residing in Zürich, Switzerland. He is the author of the book entitled *The Education of a Value Investor*.

A MEDAL WOULD BE NICE!

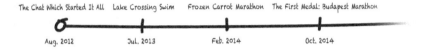

After recovering from my solitary marathon adventure, I kept thinking that I should perhaps run an official marathon, too. My motivation was totally irrational: I had never received a medal before and I had really wanted to earn one since I was little. Maybe that could have proven to me that I was not the weak, funny-looking, skinny kid after all, as my mother made me feel when convincing me to wear XXL-sized T-shirts, saying that at least they made me look halfway decent.

Parents May Well Have the Best of Intentions, But...

It is said in most personal development courses that we ought to forgive our parents and accept that no matter what they might have done when we were children, they always did the best they could for us at any given moment. It is possible that they were not ready to have children, so the "they always did the best they could for us" explanation is not easy to accept, but, in most cases, parents do not want anything bad for their children.[2] But, just to shock you a little: They might not want a whole lot of good, either!

Allan Pease, a famous body language expert, said the following at a presentation in Budapest in 2013: "If you follow your family's advice, you'll end up doing nothing, since they will regard both your successes and failures as something bad." Sound harsh? Just think about it! What your family will best handle is that if you stay on the same level where they are, neither surpassing nor falling much below them. The question is whether you want the same. (I know someone who was unable to further his education because his father would not have been able to live with the fact that his son was going to amount to more than he did. This behavior had a profoundly negative effect on the son's career path and this example is just one of many.)

Even if parents want the best for their children in all respects, they still use certain widespread ways to *direct* them, which, when embedded in their children's behavioral patterns, will produce very interesting effects later. Let me show you a few examples:

1. **Be perfect!** Parents do not really know how to handle mistakes – those always have to be corrected. Their perpetual striving for perfection discourages experiments, amputates the willingness to make mistakes, and, as a result, the ability to learn from them. Consequently, most children develop an innate fear of failure very early, which kills their ability to dive into the unknown and their courage to try new things.

2. **Hurry up!** Taking one's time just doesn't seem to be an option. Have you tied your shoes yet? Can we get going already? Parents don't realize that the nonstop drive

---

[2] Susan Forward wrote a great book about the exceptions entitled *Toxic Parents*.

Confessions of an Ironman

they enforce will prevent us from developing the ability to be in the now as adults, and instead, we are constantly looking ahead, focusing our attention on the next thing to do. We don't even take a moment to celebrate what has actually been done, as that would simply slow us down. Those who function this way can only feel safe when they are on the run pursuing something because this is the only way of living that they know.

3. **Make an effort!** Effortless successes are not usually appreciated. Results that come easy are generally not valued by people.

4. **Please others!** No matter what you do, always make sure those around you approve of it. The problem is, what you may need or want ends up being neglected.

5. **Be strong!** Do not show your real emotions because as long as you keep them hidden, no one can hurt you. "Are you crying? What kind of a man are you?" "Boys don't cry!" "Take it like a man!"

None of the above are my thoughts and neither did I become a psychologist all of a sudden. I reference Dr. Éva Kígyós' seminar entitled *Change Your Fate*, which I attended in 2013. The first task was for participants to identify which one from the list of five above is affecting their lives at the moment. When I chose all five, feeling that I was the perfect example for every one of them, I was kindly reminded that it was important to pick just one. (Naturally, it is possible that none of the above are applicable to you. They all got me thinking, that is for sure.)

Though parents mean well, they may not have the necessary level of awareness to be able to foresee the consequences of their words decades down the line. Even if done unintentionally, those words can easily inflict substantial harm. Psychologists say that our actions are directed from within, by our own 1 to

A Medal Would Be Nice!

2-year-old self, who is insistent upon reaching for solutions that have proven to work at that early age. It is highly recommended to give this some thought if you are striving to improve the quality of your life.

When I started college at eighteen, I picked up karate again in Budapest with one important condition: I told the sensei that I would not compete and that I only wanted to build myself back up to the same level I was before, and then progress from there. He seemed sympathetic. Still, a few months later, I found myself in a tournament fighting for the club. I was a promising talent and I just had to do it, plus the team needed one more member. The tournament was held in Salgótarján, the town where I was born, and there weren't too many opponents in my weight category of sub 130 (or maybe it was sub 120) pounds. The brown- and black-belted guys were obviously better than I, but, by some miracle, I managed to take the third step on the podium. My long-lived dream was going to be realized – I was finally going to get a medal!

When it was all over, they lined us up at the podium for the medal ceremony by category. When they reached me, I was regretfully informed that they ran out of bronze medals, but they assured me I would eventually get a certificate. There went my medal! Despite earning it, I still did not receive it. The truth of the matter was that I didn't really feel I actually deserved it, as there were only a few less experienced competitors that I had to defeat for it. Still, it would have been nice though.

Overcompensation and Self-reflection

I just could not live without having a medal; I ended up severely overcompensating when it comes to collecting finisher medals. I signed up for some competitions just to get the unique medals they were handing out. I was able to examine myself

Confessions of an Ironman

and recognize these thoughts and the connected feelings so that they didn't control me from deep within. This process, called self-reflection, is a very useful *technique*. It is wise to take a moment and step back before making important decisions, distance yourself from the emotions they evoke, and ask: "Why do I want this? What is my real motivation behind it?" Most of the time, what is longed for is none other than a feeling; when you recognize that, it is worth taking the time to think about whether there is a different way for you to spark that feeling without the given goal. (I must confess, I had not gone through these steps before the Ironman simply because I was not at that level of consciousness back then.)

Following the tournament, my karate coach's next move is a good illustration of how *harmonious* a relationship we had. He sent me a letter; he could not spell my name or the name of the street where I lived, not to mention that what he had to say was not the least bit to my liking. He had an ingenious idea to identify attack combinations with code numbers for the next contest. He sent me information to memorize so that I would do what he wanted when he shouted the secret codes from the side of the mat, he explained. That was precisely the sort of brainless, robotic approach that I could never identify with. Since I still did not want to compete and this guy had trouble even writing my name down, my return to karate was cut short. From then on, sports were out of the picture – until the previously mentioned traumatic city track run.

When I learned that marathon athletes didn't need to finish on the podium in order to get something hung around their necks, I could not help thinking that I had found my thing. I would get myself ready for the 2014 Budapest Marathon in October, and I would finally get my very first medal. Get, I say? No, I would earn it! The pocket-tyrant Nike app was getting reinstalled, let the preparation begin!

As I recall, the training went smoothly. I don't remember anything extraordinary, but the day of the race is very clear in my memory.

A Medal Would Be Nice!

Being a complete beginner, I chose – _very sensibly_ – a marathon as my very first organized running race. Lacking any experience, as the mass of people started moving at the start signal, I got carried away and ran with them, not suspecting that it would come back to bite me. I went with the momentum and kept passing runners around me. In spite of the October date, it was an unusually warm day, which made things a bit complicated for me. I don't remember exactly how far into the race I was when I got completely spent, but there was still a lot left to go when I ended up having to stop at a few aid stations. My overall finishing time was 4 hours and 8 minutes, and I did receive the first medal of my life. To be honest, however, it was not as satisfying as I expected it to be. I did not like the medal _(it is still one of the ugliest pieces in my collection)_, neither did I like that I could not complete the race without walking. Collapsing onto the grass in the finishers' area, the thought of _"never again"_ did not come as a surprise.

Today, having gone through multiple attempts, I am fully aware of the contrast in how you feel when you complete a marathon and hit the sweet spot, running a steady pace all the way through, as opposed to going out too hard in the beginning of the race and merely surviving a good chunk of the second half. Truth be told, it took me six attempts before I was able to run the marathon at a steady pace, which only happened after I did the Ironman.

The medal was in the bag and, more importantly, I had now successfully ticked off two Ironman disciplines. After the endurance swim, the completion of an official full marathon gave me enough self-confidence to believe that I was capable of going the distance. Right around that time, I saw on Facebook that an acquaintance of mine had been preparing for the Ironman and had just completed the Austria Triathlon Podersdorf full-distance race. It seemed to me I had done all I could on my own, and I needed help. The time had come to talk to someone who had actually been where I was going. His advice, and a good pitcher of beer, might point me in the right direction.

II. ALONE AGAINST THE WORLD

A DREAM OR A GOAL?

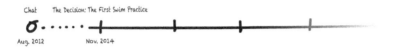

Dani was willing to meet, even if we needed to dig around a little to clarify how we *knew* each other. We met in a billiards bar called Typhoon in Budapest. Since Dani drove, instead of having a few cold ones, we ended up drinking mineral water while I learned about some of the essentials (going by the notes on my phone, we met on October 19, 2014).

One piece of good advice I received was that if I was serious about wanting to do an Ironman but couldn't swim freestyle, I should start working on that as soon as possible, since it would take me at least a year and a half to execute that technique in the pool. I also received a few good pointers on what to look for when buying a bike. That could not be put off much longer, either. I was completely in the dark on that front, so I took some quick notes on a mobile app, which I did not even look at for months. It was enough for me to know what should come next: I had to start my lessons with a swimming instructor and then I had to start attending regular triathlon swim practices. The notion of being in the water was still daunting, so having to put that on public display made me very uncomfortable, to say the least.

Even though I had their number, I decided to e-mail the warmly recommended swim coach ladies (even that took me a week after our talk with Dani), and I was not at all upset that there was no reply to my inquiry for a few more weeks. As it turned out, the ladies accidentally sent the replies meant for me to each other instead, so I still ended up having to make a call to arrange for my first proper swim lesson. There was no way to avoid taking a few private lessons from one of the coaches since I could not do the freestyle stroke at all. The plan was that after 6-7 sessions, I would be able to execute the technique more or less properly; after that, I could join the regular practices three times a week with the triathlon team.

I regard November, 2014, to be the time when my irrevocable decision was made: I will complete an Ironman. Could there be any other reason to make myself get out of bed in the wee hours to make it to practice sessions starting at 6 a.m., in the cold and dark of winter, just so that I could crawl into the similarly cold water and suffer through an hour, three times a week, nearly drowning the whole time? My plan lacked a timeline in the beginning so, according to the general interpretation made by the success gurus of the West, it did not qualify as a real goal, but was merely a dream. Later, in the midst of all the trainings, a thought popped into my head about that. It may prove to be of interest, so I will share it now.

"Dream First, Plan Later!"

The following words kept flashing before my eyes during a creek run: *Dream first, plan later!* "What does it all mean?" I asked myself. On that particular day, I had plenty of time to think, still having a long way to go. The Western success trainings tell us that if we do not set a deadline when aiming for a goal, it will simply remain a dream; referring to it as a real objective is just self-delusion.

The problem with this approach, in my opinion, is that if it becomes an ingrained practice and you stick to it all the time, you disconnect from your creativity entirely. Your inner child

Confessions of an Ironman

will not have the courage to dream, because, as an adult, you will silence all inspiration coming from it, thinking that you wouldn't be able to set a rational execution plan to go with the ideas it sparks, as the Western-style success recipes would like you to do. Or perhaps you would, but the fact is that you are afraid to, because that sort of thing could stir up your life too much, and you'd rather find ways to avoid any complications. As for avoidance, they are always plenty of ways: You oppress the creativity that is deeply rooted in you from your childhood. You stop dreaming as you silence those voices, and you stick to the strictly rational realm that is bound by thoughts and ideas you deem feasible, ultimately, closing yourself into a narrower world. And this will eventually make you feel miserable.

What is the solution? For me, the "dream first, plan later" approach worked well in connection with the Ironman (and other things, too). If some success guru had convinced me that I needed to have a detailed game plan first, with ideal timings and deadlines identified, then it's highly likely I would have targeted a much smaller goal than the Ironman, as that would have been much easier to work toward. I say dive in and try disregarding the Western wonder recipes in the beginning, which were not known to you when you were a child anyways, mind you, yet you still reached your goals! *(Toys, treats...ring a bell? I'm sure you got most of what you really wanted, even though you did not make a list of those goals and chanted them as a means of affirmation.)* Once you are able to shake off all your learned disabilities, it is time to let your imagination soar and dream with your inner child's freedom! Nothing stands in your way – you can write down anything and you don't have to know the *Hows* and the *Whens*! You want to become a billionaire? You want to travel the world? It does not matter what you put down; if at least once in your life – unlike most people – you let your inner child take the driver's seat, a truly unique dream list will be revealed.

A Dream or a Goal?

How many people do you think have such a list? Out of those closest to me, I am certain that nobody does. Why? Because most people are wrapped in an "it's just not realistic" mindset. Very few dare to dream nowadays. Just look around, it is written on so many faces! Multitudes of gray, uninspired lives that completely lack aspiration. It's a shame because everyone should have dreams...

I had a medal display made where I could keep the growing selection of my "precious ones." I had it engraved with a Walt Disney quote: "If you can dream it, you can do it!" You are capable of anything that you can visualize in your mind, but since this is not meant to be a spiritual book, my heart tells me to turn back to the three-step goal realization recipe, which was the byproduct of the drawing course.

Once your dreams take shape, you can start brainstorming what the first steps might be in making them a reality. That may be as simple as reading a book or writing an e-mail you have been hesitating to write. It is perfectly okay if you don't see right away how to break down a seemingly farfetched goal into a bunch of rational and justifiable steps. The important thing is to have an idea about what the very next small step could be on the road to achieving it. Once you have that, you can surely get started, and your subconscious will guide you down the path to the final destination. I would like to add that I don't really believe in a *"leaving it all to spirituality and that will get me to the finish line"* solution, expecting to reach a goal by merely floating on an unconsciously attracted chain of events. Letting it happen as it comes is not the answer in my experience; I had to work very hard for everything I achieved. However, I found, on countless occasions, that once I set my mind to something, the solutions and tools which could get me closer to that goal crossed my path eventually. You tend to notice those signals, leads, or pieces of

Confessions of an Ironman

> information which, for one reason or another, are important to you. Don't you think that if you truly let your inner child's spirit free and, with that guidance, you make a list of your dreams, there will be so many emotions involved that you become more sensitive to noticing things that cross your path that could help you achieve those dreams? You just need to be willing to recognize them.

The Ironman represented a totally unattainable and incredibly enormous goal for me. (Just like the financial freedom I dreamed about when I was living in a lower middle-class concrete jungle in the countryside – and which I still achieved at a young age.) I had no idea how to map it out to see each step leading to completion. However, once I mustered up the courage to take the first step and started my journey, I was always able to come up with the *very next step* that I needed to take. These may be as simple as sitting down with Dani or writing an e-mail to the swim coaches. The path to success is made up of these sorts of small strides. Just try not to sentence your dreams to death right at their birth! Dare to dream - you can mull over the details later!

The Ironman preparation led me to many similarly interesting notions. Most of the time they were simply "handed to me" in vivid clarity. Sort of like a flash, they just popped into my head out of the blue, and I usually had plenty of time to unwrap their meaning. *(The 15-20 training hours that I undertook every week toward the end of my preparation gave me lots of time to think.)* I cannot explain where these flashes came from – that's not even important – and I certainly cannot answer why they sometimes appeared in the form of witty proverbs.

After meeting with Dani, the only bridge over the vast pit separating the Ironman dream from becoming a rational goal was something he had told me. According to him, I could possibly tackle a half

A Dream or a Goal?

Ironman[3] in the following year, meaning 2015. The real Ironman might be possible after that, in 2016, if I trained properly. I can't say I was able to identify with that timeline immediately; instead, my focus remained on the next small step. I just wanted to get to my first swimming lesson, make it through without looking like a complete fool, and then get home. Later, while in the midst of my near-drowning acts in the pool, I frequently remembered what I wrote in my e-mail looking to sign up at the triathlon club:

"Currently, I can only do the breaststroke, but I would like to do an Ironman later, so I need to learn the freestyle."

"I am sure everyone drops the bomb saying they want to do an Ironman, then they quit halfway there," I thought. "I, on the other hand, will not do that – even if I cannot cross the pool in freestyle." These were the sort of things that kept my thoughts occupied during the first few months (!), as I was unable to cross it, indeed.

Mesi, one of the swim coaches at the triathlon club, taught me the basics of the freestyle stroke in about 6-7 lessons. The best thing she told me was "don't worry, everyone has to start somewhere." With that, she put me somewhat at ease. Until hearing that, all I thought was that I'd be joining professional triathletes at a swimming practice with a death sentence pinned to my forehead since I was unable to complete even half of the first exercise code-named "400 IM warm-up."[4]

All in all, the private lessons went well. At the first session, Mesi asked me to swim a lap to show her how I usually swim. My "usual" choice was the breaststroke, so it was obvious what she was going to see. Then, following this warm-up exercise, she shrunk my spirits a little when she asked, "Is this it? Alright, let's clean this up a bit

---

[3] The half Ironman (or the 70.3 in the Ironman-branded race circuit) is a race over half the distances of the full Ironman triathlon. It consists of a 1.2-mile swim, a 56-mile bike ride and a 13.1-mile run.
[4] Butterfly, backstroke, breaststroke, and freestyle (front crawl), alternating strokes for 400 meters.

Confessions of an Ironman

before we move onto anything else." So much for having a stable foundation.

Those who learned freestyle as an adult won't be surprised that it took enormous effort for me to make it across the pool in the beginning. For months, my freestyle speed was painfully slower than my breaststroke, on top of which my attempts exhausted me beyond belief. To make things even worse, I often had suffocating thoughts while swimming, reminding me of my fear of water, urging me to just get out and quit. This didn't make things easier when learning the proper technique or when trying to correct any mistakes. Truth is, no words of mine could describe the hydrophobic feeling of suffocating panic that I felt. You'll have to imagine the kinds of thoughts one might wake up with before dawn, in the biting cold of winter, so that he can cross half the town by bus and then get into a pool, while terrified to his core, and which fear he must suppress in order to get closer to a seemingly unattainable goal. It was not pleasant to be in my company around that time – especially on the evenings before swimming practice.

Mesi usually gave me homework to complete between our private lessons, which meant that I could return to the place where I prepared for the lake crossing, the BVSC city pool. With my "more than lacking" skills and a prescribed list of various self-torture drills, I was ready to put on some real authentic shows. Occasionally, it even felt like I was beginning to do fairly well with certain drills, but when I stopped at the wall, I always discovered that while the other lanes were jampacked in the 25-meter pool, I, on the other hand, had the lane all to myself. Clearly, I wasn't such a badass that the amateur swimmers would empty a lane just for me as soon as I made my eminent appearance – no, I had to work very hard to earn that privilege! I think those involved must have thought that seeing someone drown would not be very pleasant, so when I started training (let's call it that), every swimmer whose fate brought them to the same pool at the same time decided that it was best to be as far away from my struggle as possible. Going by the smiles of the lifeguard, I was sure he recognized me, and he had to have

A Dream or a Goal?

been able to envision my bright swimming future. The one-armed butterfly is an ambitious swim drill, especially for one who is not even familiar with the basics, but if I get an assignment, I complete it, no matter what – I asked for it, after all.

Mesi told me that she could tell I had been practicing. According to her, not many others hit the pool on their own, even though she always asked them to. After 6-7 private lessons and the horror show practice sessions I put in at the BVSC pool, I was pronounced ready for real combat by early December: I could join the proper triathlon swimming practices. To celebrate my advancement, Mesi quickly took a trip to the other side of the globe and did not have to witness my premier. It was wise of her to do so.

My fear of the private lessons was nothing compared to the way I felt about the team practices – I was straight-out terrified of them. My only memory of the first session is that I swallowed what seemed to be an unthinkable amount of water while struggling for survival. Ákos' merciful comment – he was the main coach – was simply this: "It wasn't too bad for a first one." It did not shock me at all that I could not execute the technique perfectly after a few weeks' practice, On the other hand, I was devastated by the state of my fitness, which was made painfully clear on that swim adventure. My endurance was nowhere near what I thought it was. Having completed the marathon, I was convinced that I didn't need to worry about making it through any of the swim trainings. After one lousy length of the pool, however, I was gasping for air, and there was not a chance that I could go on without stopping.

Expensive Gadgets as a Means for Motivation

When I was done with the private lessons and started the regular practice sessions, I decided it was time to purchase a proper sports watch as a sign of my solid commitment. After a little research, I chose a Garmin Forerunner 920XT – a model that had

Confessions of an Ironman

> just come out on the market. It had all the bells and whistles, and it was evident that I would not be able to use most of the functions – the obvious reasons being that I did not yet own a bike and I could hardly swim. The way I saw it, it was already a huge step for me not to have to use my phone on my runs. As for the rest of the functions, I assumed I would gradually build up to them.
>
> The role of the watch was mainly to strengthen my commitment (if for no other reason than its hefty price tag), and when I wore it, I felt that leaving a session incomplete was simply not an option. I hardly ever used the sharing option it has – I am not one to flood Facebook with my training session details. The simple fact that it records all my training data and makes my progress trackable is motivating enough in itself. Any small thing that blows wind in one's sail is helpful with goals of this magnitude.

Realizing that my progress was too slow, I dusted off my imaginary collection of suicidal training methods and decided to pay a visit to BVSC over the weekend, where the 50-meter pool was scheduled to be open for the public. (*"Just what I need,"* I thought. *"That will surely give me room for self-expression."*) The task was clear: "I am going to swim 1500 meters, freestyle, without finding any excuses this time, leaving my self-suffocation tantrums out of the picture." I arrived around lunchtime. Walking down the deck, my eyes met those of the lifeguard. His memories had to have faded somewhat since I had not made any appearances there for weeks. He gave me the impression he was about to leave to grab something to eat, but then paused and turned back. It must have crossed his mind that he'd better stay and keep watch.

Without further hesitation, I began the 30 laps. After starting with relaxed strokes, my breathing gradually became less and less smooth. Finally, a feeling of total exhaustion came over me and I

A Dream or a Goal?

had to stop – I was precisely halfway across the pool. I quickly went to grab the wall on the side – I knew better than to pick an inside lane for my stunt. As I was catching my breath, I noticed that the lifeguard was still there, watching with an expression on his face that said, *"lunch is postponed,"* because from what he could tell so far, *"anything could happen here."* Little did he know that I had 29 and a half lengths of the pool left to go! Fully aware that a lot is dependent upon how one is framing a given task, I told myself there were *only* 29 and a half lengths left to go.

I had to stop at the end of each 50-meter lap because I could hardly breathe. After the short rest stops, I could make it to about half of every length, but from then on I fought a life-and-death battle for the remaining tens of meters. Despite all that, it was never a question that I would complete what I came for. Looking back now, of course, and considering my fitness level then, it is obvious that I bit off more than I could chew. In the meantime, this little adventure (*what else could I call any of my similarly insane ideas?*) helped me break down the barriers I built in my head, and push my limits further out, strengthening the thought in my head that if I was able to go through with this, then I should also be able to go through those training sessions without stopping all the time. This was an important milestone in my development.

Adri, another coach at the club, once told me that endurance takes a lot of sweat and time to develop, yet it can be lost very quickly. After realizing that I was nowhere near where I hoped to be in that regard, in spite of all the effort I put in working up to the marathon, the months to follow were strictly about working on the fundamentals of my swim technique. It took me months to remain somewhat calm getting on that bus early in the morning to get to the pool. My case, I think, was very unique, because when Anikó decided to pick up swimming, it only took her two or three occasions to come home smiling after her sessions. "What could they be doing at the other pool, where she swims?" I wondered.

Confessions of an Ironman

My first swim time trial was on March 20, 2015. I skipped two prior trials – one because of a trip to Dubai, and the other because I had a late-night meeting with some friends. The truth is, they freaked me out because I would have to swim 400 meters without stopping, maintaining a steady pace – none of which I could have done back then. At my first go, I managed to cover the intimidating distance in 9 minutes and 19 seconds, which at least gave a reference point to track my future progress. Although I was not particularly proud of my time, I was definitely proud of not fleeing from the challenge. There was not a whole lot to celebrate though – nor was there any time to do so, as I was already deeply preoccupied with an event coming up on the 22nd of March.

WHAT A PRETTY MEDAL! HAVE YOU BEEN TO ROME?

Despite swimming three times a week, the first few months went by without any significant changes in the way I moved in the pool. I did notice that I was less and less short of breath and, swimming at a pace reasonable for my level, I was gradually able to complete the entire training sessions. Based on what Dani had told me, I figured this program wouldn't change much for about a year and a half, until my freestyle became stable. I needed something more to keep me busy.

Since I did not have a bike (according to the receipt I dug up, I didn't purchase one until February, 2015), I was left with running. Looking through a flashy runner's magazine, an unusual medal caught my attention, and I immediately knew I just had to have it. I quickly learned from the ad that it was the finisher medal for a marathon in Rome, scheduled for March, 2015. I was in luck; convincing a woman to go along for a quick visit to Rome was not too difficult, especially since Anikó and I had never been there before. Needless to say, she was in without hesitation. She actually decided she would sign up also and complete her very first marathon there.

Confessions of an Ironman

The preparation was uneventful. Since I only swam with the triathletes at that point – who I don't think had any idea whether I did anything else besides that – my running workouts were guided by the Nike app once again. The reason I take time to share this Roman excursion is that it was during this marathon preparation when I first felt I could easily keep an 8 minute per mile pace on my creek runs and didn't get nearly as fatigued as before, when I actually ran much slower. Each small advancement I made in the pool had a detectable effect on my running. I was very happy about this, since it was around this time when I first felt that *I actually liked running.* This is to say that I felt that running had nested itself in my heart to remain with me for life, even if I wasn't working toward a special goal that involved it. (This was quite a contrast to what I felt after suffering through the majority of the second half of the Budapest Marathon, thinking *"I will finish somehow and this suffering will end."*)

> *"We may train or peak for a certain race,*
> *but running is a lifetime sport."*
> *Alberto Salazar, world-class long-distance*
> *runner and coach*

Although the first months of the year were extremely cold for a marathon preparation by the creek, conditions like that hadn't stopped me before. *(See my frozen carrot marathon adventure.)* I enjoyed the training and my new-found strength so much that, for no particular reason, I ran a sub 4-hour marathon (3 hours 47 minutes) during one of the sessions prior to a swimming practice the next morning. The count of my completions of the full running distance had reached three, with only one finish in an official event. My goal for Rome was a sub 4-hour time, but I also nurtured a secret hope of finishing under 3 hours 40 minutes. I even promised a friend that if I succeeded, I would bring him a bottle of his favorite Italian wine.

What a Pretty Medal! Have You Been to Rome?

As if completing a marathon was not difficult enough, I managed to catch some sort of stomach infection a few weeks before the race. I couldn't keep anything down and lived on a mix of doctor-prescribed minerals. I did manage to keep up with my weekly mileage quotas, although the pace and feeling were far from desirable, not to mention my state of mind! When I expressed my slight skepticism whether a simple diet would resolve the problem, my family practitioner, being the funny guy he is, simply told me that I better let my body take its time to heal, otherwise he might have to order a gastroscopy, along with a few similarly inviting sounding examinations. He convinced me! I went with basically not eating anything for days.

You can imagine what it was like visiting friends in Jászberény for a cookout where wursts and sausages were the main fare on the menu. I was a miserable spectator while they were eating and drinking. They also posed the question why I decided to pick a city for a marathon, which, according to our Latin studies, was built on seven hills. Oops, I missed that little detail! That meant I should expect a hilly course, right? Be that as it may, I would do it, no matter what.

I felt more or less healthy by race day, so the only thing that bothered me was getting soaked in the pouring rain even before the race started. Rome is a beautiful city and the route was spectacular. I only recall one hilly section, but I remember long sections of cobblestone streets that were quite dangerous because it was difficult to negotiate the holes where the stones were missing. The rain filled up those mini craters and it was all up to chance how many times I stepped in them. I felt good and everything went as planned until around mile 23; from there I had to fight through the final miles to end up with a 3-hour and 36-minute time engraved into the dream medal while I waited for Anikó to finish.

I felt good about this run until I heard months later at running practice that a steady pace is the most ideal for a marathon. I reevaluated

Confessions of an Ironman

my initial take on my performance and came to the conclusion that there were still some bits here and there where I could hone my *"I start out, let the momentum take me until I nearly fall apart, then hang on desperately and hope to finish somehow"* approach.

At any rate, after Rome, I was convinced that I would have no problems with the run in the Ironman, or, I should say, I felt that the run was the discipline I was best prepared for. Besides that, I especially enjoyed the combination of traveling and sightseeing, wrapped in a sport-experience, along with the great vibes, so I started seriously thinking about perhaps running some more marathons in various places around the world. It seemed that could be a wonderful adventure without the less-than-constructive feelings of self-punishment. By that time, however, a brand-new bike had been sitting in my living room for some weeks, and the uneasy feeling that I should be doing something about that was growing...

THIS BIKE WAS WAITING FOR ME!

Many months had passed since the conversation with Dani. I had started swimming, the running question was answered, but as one of my friends had so eloquently pointed out during our entertaining chat years before, "For the Ironman, one has to have a bike, too." Looking through my notes taken at the mineral water talk, I was under the impression that I couldn't go wrong with a Merida bicycle, which, considering the distance I would be traveling, should be equipped with at least a "serious entry-level" groupset. Dani suggested the Shimano Tiagra set because it was unlikely that I would want to spend more. This was the information I went by when I set out on the hunt for my Merida-Tiagra combo.

In early 2015, I took notice of a few adverts promoting a big sale on the previous year's models. Unfortunately, I was so uncomfortable with the whole bike shopping process that I put it off until February. When I finally made it to the retailer, they told me that I was a little late and the last of the stock had just been taken. I, on the other hand, cool as a cucumber, pointed at a Merida bike hanging on the wall and asked, "How about that one?!" It was the very last one of the previous year's models. As the sales assistant started his questioning, "What size are you looking for?" the story got interesting. "Do you mean a numerical or letter size designation?" I responded, having no clue how sizing was marked on bikes.

Since it was clear we didn't speak a common language, the bike quickly came down off the wall and, after measuring it up to me,

Confessions of an Ironman

we (or rather the sales guy) came to the conclusion that it might just be a good fit. "It's got a Tiagra gruppo – will that do for you?" came the next question. At least this one I could answer, because the remaining inquiries – such as "Do you need an SPD pedal[5]?" – made my near-complete ignorance undeniable since I did not have the faintest idea what was being asked. When the sales assistant learned that I had only ridden an old Russian steel horse and a mass-produced Wal-Mart-level mountain bike, he strongly recommended taking the bike with traditional pedals and also urged me to buy a helmet immediately, as it was almost certain, given that I had never been on a bike like that before, that I would crash a few times.

The last model on sale was mine. I had to wait a few days before I could pick it up because they had to make a few adjustments to it, which was just enough time for me to think it through and decide that it would probably not be a very good idea to make the long trip home through Budapest my first ride, since I could not even keep it on a semi-straight line on a closed, flat test road. Basically, I had no idea how to handle the bike, therefore I thought it best to make its first outing a trip home in the trunk of my car.

Nevertheless, according to my Garmin stats, I took it out for about a 7-mile test spin that day. During that ride I learned that I was a high risk to both myself and others on the road. I couldn't even steer the bicycle properly. Not to mention that I could hardly breathe after only a few hundred meters, despite my swimming and marathon background. It was clear that cycling would be yet another type of exercise I would need getting used to.

---

[5] SPD stands for "Shimano Pedaling Dynamics." This is a clipless pedaling system. It uses a cleat that is fastened to the sole of the bike shoe which snaps into the pedal, enabling the rider to not only push down but also to apply a pulling force on the pedals while riding.

I PICKED OUT THE
IDEAL FIRST "RACE"

Following the Rome Marathon, I was in need of something that forced me to carry on. I needed a goal that was both rationally feasible but for which I had to work hard. I decided I would sign up for the very first triathlon of my life, despite the fact that I hadn't yet spent any time on my bike.

I definitely wanted a short event for my first triathlon, but the version officially called sprint distance did not appeal to me. The term "sprint" gave me the feeling it was the sort of race where the intensity was painfully high, precisely what I did not want for my first triathlon experience.

The next step up, the Olympic or standard distance, captured my attention. Basically, I was convinced that I would not have any problems with the 1500-meter swim or the 40-kilometer (25 miles) bike ride; as for the latter, I was completely oblivious to what I considered a totally manageable distance. The 10K run was something I could pull out of my hat any time or anywhere, beyond any doubt. All I wanted to do is finish. I especially liked the slogan of the event, which was held in a lakeside town called Velence: "*This isn't a race, rather a station on your journey – a pleasurable triathlon where you can test it all.*" All in all, it seemed like the perfect event

Confessions of an Ironman

for a first-timer. Still, I did not rush to sign up. First I had to make friends with my new roommate, my bike.

I began riding in April, 2015, without the slightest understanding of how to go about it properly. It took me months to figure out that I was riding completely different from the others, using only the highest gears. The way I saw it, I was preparing for a triathlon, which is nothing but tough, and tough guys must use tough gears and leave the shifting to the softies. (Later I heard a funny phrase: "Shifting is the weapon of the weak ones." My way of thinking at the time, precisely.) I didn't even know that variables such as pedaling cadence existed; I would never have figured them out on my own. It was only later that I bombarded Ákos, who was "lucky-enough" to lead my Ironman preparation, with my greenhorn questions.

So, there I was, in April, knowing that in a few weeks' time I was to perform something called cycling, and I could not even leave a traffic light on green without rolling in gigantic zig-zags.

On my less than successful first time out, I couldn't even get out of the city. I ended up spending more time standing by the bike with my phone in my hand, completely lost and searching the map of Budapest, than in the saddle. This half-hearted attempt happened on the 9th of April. I managed to cover about 20 miles in 2 hours and 11 minutes, and if I want to be absolutely honest, those GPS search stops I was forced to make saved my butt, because not only did I lack the strength for that kind of riding, but I was also scared riding in heavy traffic.

One week later, I managed to make it beyond the city limits of the capital. Dani, who also lived in the area, had suggested I take the road toward a small town named Fót. I thought if those roads were good enough for him to prepare for the Ironman, then they would surely work for me as well. I biked the same route all the time, and lacking any experience, couldn't tell whether the sections where I could hardly turn the pedals counted as proper hills or if I was simply too weak. Later, I was told that those were proper hills indeed.

I pumped out 40 km (25 miles) as early as my second ride (in 1 hour and 39 minutes), and around the end of April had the courage to push to the 50 km mark (31 miles). I always rode alone. According to my Garmin, I covered about 100 miles during my first month of biking. Keeping tabs on my speed or any other variables was way too much to worry about at that point; I still had to surmount challenges such as drinking out of a bottle or blowing my nose without having to stop. Even though I was yet to see a triathlon race, I had a strong hunch that not many participants would pull over to bust out the Kleenex, so I got into some pretty absurd experiments as to how to best solve that dilemma. The "outcome" usually ended up on my outfit, but passing cars also received a fair share of it. It took time before I felt I was somewhat in control in the saddle, and was able to think about simply gaining some speed to help me muster the courage to enter the test-triathlon.

My approach was that I would occasionally ride more than the 25 miles to build up my confidence for the race. In May, I rode over 310 miles, undertaking even 40- and 50-mile rides, which, for me, were still very long distances. Every part of my body was aching sitting on the bicycle, and I didn't even dare to think what it would be like to ride 112 miles in an Ironman race. However painful that was, what made those months memorable was something else...

CAUGHT BY THE GUARD RAIL

I don't usually take pictures of myself, but what happened on May 19, 2015, gave me the inspiration. (The date was in my phone, otherwise I would not have remembered it.) That was the first day I planned to go out for a run right after biking. Dani had mentioned that it was important to practice a few times because, initially, it can be quite a shocking experience. Now that I think about it, we

Confessions of an Ironman

discussed a lot of things over mineral water. Had we been drinking beer, perhaps I would not remember all the details.

The day's plan was to bike 30 miles after the morning swim, and then do a creek run of a bit over 8 miles. I still wasn't comfortable enough to let my thoughts wander while riding, but my general fear had subsided to a level where I wasn't tensed up with my hands tightly clenched around the handlebars the whole time. Just like when someone with a fresh driver's license is beginning to think that he's got things under control behind the wheel – that's when it gets dangerous. So, I was in that phase; on top of that, I felt deeply sorry for myself for having to go out for a run right after my ride. From one moment to the next, after going over a railroad crossing, I got startled by a car, as it got very close to me, and I jerked on the handlebars just enough to weave off onto the gravel on the shoulder. In a flash, I decided not to turn the bike back onto the pavement, thinking that if this car was so close then the next one would surely hit me if I messed up the maneuver. There was a guard rail on the other side, and that's what I hit without braking, at about 15 miles per hour. My bike stayed intact, as I turned to dampen the blow with my upper arm. Traffic stopped and one of the drivers asked me if I was sure I could get back in the saddle.

Having nearly 20 miles left to ride that day, and the run to follow, there was no question whether or not I'd carry on. From that point on, though, my hands were clamped to the handlebars while I completely ignored the huge wound on my upper arm until I got home. As I got a chance to take a better look at myself when I got home, I realized that my state was far from funny. I quickly sent a picture to Anikó with the subtitle *"blood-selfie"* so that she could be worried out of her mind while I was running. I figured the more people are touched by my project, the better...

Only the beginning of the run was difficult. I could not settle into my usual pace and it proved to be very demanding to make the shift from one type of motion to the other. This transition clearly needed more getting used to, so I decided to do another 30+6-mile combo shortly thereafter. I had to, since I was pressed for time, plus I knew nothing about how to construct a consciously designed training plan yet.

Ironically, my little collision happened just a few days after I signed up for my first triathlon. This triggered those spiritually more sensitive around me to point out that my accident was a sign that I shouldn't be doing this to myself, and that I should not punish myself with a triathlon simply because I didn't believe I was good enough. In hindsight, their viewpoint had a lot of truth to it, which I also came to realize on multiple occasions during my Ironman training. There was only one thing those realizations could not change though: I had already made my decision. I had decided that I was going to become an Ironman. From that point on, there were only two possible outcomes in my book: Either I do it or something makes it totally impossible for me to do it. I can be reasoned with before I make a decision, but after it is made, I will keep on going relentlessly. until I accomplish whatever I have set my mind to. (It isn't seldom that this attitude of mine makes those around me crazy.)

FROM THE SWIMMING POOL TO THE HOSPITAL

The marks on my arm from the bike crash were visible for months, but that didn't disturb me nearly as much as what I experienced a few days after the accident. I hit the guard rail with my right side and I could hardly use that hand. It was as if all the strength had been sucked right out of it. First, I didn't really let that bother me, but two days after the collision when I was reminded at practice that I ought to close my fingers while swimming, I got a bit alarmed. My ring and pinky fingers had apparently decided to live independent lives. No matter how hard I tried, I could not make them line up with my middle finger as I tried to close them. After several feeble attempts at home, I decided that this should probably be looked at, even though I was not a frequent visitor at the doctor's office.

Confessions of an Ironman

I called the nearest hospital, where I was told that the next available appointment with the doctor I needed to see was in a couple of weeks. This statement provoked a slight change in my tone and I told the receptionist that one of my hands was not moving. Since I'd rather not wait for weeks with this problem, I told her I would be at the hospital in exactly twenty minutes. All she said was that I should bring along a really thick book because there was a long line waiting to see a doctor.

Indeed, the wait was long enough to read a few hundred pages before I got in to see the specialist, who was immediately baffled that I hadn't yet been sent to get x-rayed in so many hours. We had been studying how weak my fingers were for a while when he asked me, *"Have you been in any sort of accident recently?"* When I told him the guard rail story, he had me remove my T-shirt at once. He looked at the sizable and quite colorful scab and managed to ask, *"Do you suspect a connection between the two things?"* After clarifying that I was clearly incapable of drawing the apparent parallel between the two things, he informed me that the impact had damaged the nerves responsible for the coordination of the fingers in question. His recommendation: I should go home and wait a few weeks and the problem would fix itself. While I was immensely relieved hearing that, from that moment on, I completely ruled out the option of ever seeing a doctor again. I made myself one with *"the problem will fix itself"* approach.

During the final stage of my triathlon preparation, I managed to make it to a sports store about 5 minutes before closing to purchase a wetsuit. The water temperature of Lake Velence at that time of year clearly called for it. They stayed open a "bit" late to assist me, and the transaction was a success. I also requested a flash tutorial before a swim practice by the pool to get somewhat up to speed on what kinds of things I should pack for a triathlon race, what a transition[6] was like, and, basically, to find out if there was anything else I ought to know before hitting the road. After that, I felt ready, at least in theory. I managed to pile up about 500 miles on the bike leading up to the June 7th race, and I did not see any reason why I should not be able to complete an Olympic distance course. The two other disciplines, swimming and running, should not pose any problems.

---

[6] Transition is the change from one sport to the next during the race. It is also called T1 and T2, respectively. T1 is the first one, from swim to bike, and T2 is the second one, from bike to run.

THERE GOES MY TRIATHLON VIRGINITY, THE NIGHT AFTER A WEDDING

We arrived at the lake the day before the race. Right after checking into our hotel, I headed down to the water for a test swim. I had never tried my freestyle in open water before. I was all over the place, clearly unable to swim from buoy to buoy in a straight line, not to mention I couldn't see anything, which made it impossible to orient myself. I learned very quickly that it was nothing like swimming in a pool and perhaps it would have been a good idea to put in some open water practice as well; by then, it was too late. The water was comfortable and the organizers didn't allow the use of wetsuits the next day. My little swim test just added to the list of my worries. Assuming that my watch measured the distance I covered in the lake accurately, it seemed questionable whether I would be able to complete the 1500 meters inside the official time limit. While I found this hard to believe, the figures seemed unmistakable.

Fortunately, I didn't have much time to fret over my plight because we were expected at a wedding that evening. It was a perfect prelude to the very first triathlon of my life. I tried hard to eat and drink with moderation and we left right after midnight so I could get some sleep before the big day. Truth is, my self-imposed restraint made me feel like I was really screwing with myself with the whole triathlon business. To top it all off, the bride remarked as we were leaving, "Triathlon?! Gosh, that is the toughest!" That comment managed to deepen my self-pity even further.

Self-pity or Addiction to Approbation? Two Strange Energy Bars

According to Tony Robbins' teaching, as I mentioned before, we have two innate fears which have profound effects on our lives. The first one is the feeling of "I am not good enough," which is rooted in our inability to function on our own as infants, and in that our later childhood is also lived in dependency on the adults around us. On our own, we are simply not good enough.

The second one, which is the basic fear that "I will not be loved," is closely connected to the first one. We learned as infants that if we cry when we feel pain, then we receive attention and love as an immediate reaction. Since our inner child is also present in our adulthood, we often complain because crying has worked before, and through it we received the love we desired. Complaining and self-pity are like energy bars: They give you energy as long as you have an audience to pour your complaints and self-pity on.

When we take our first steps as we begin to walk, our environment celebrates, we are showered with rewards, positive reactions, and love. The feelings evoked by this feedback are deeply ingrained in us and we do everything in our power to keep receiving similar love. We can go on living our lives like that without limit: We can run marathons, do Ironman triathlons, and let's not leave out the ever so important Facebook posts to go with them, so that we can harvest the well-deserved attention, praise, and love in return for our efforts.

Confessions of an Ironman

The wedding ended up being the most advantageous prelude. For a long time, the race in Velence was the only one where I actually put in a good night's sleep the night before the race. (Perhaps, I should have had a bottle of wine before the other ones as well.) In the morning, after pumping my tires up as hard as a rock, I took off to the race center, with a sizable, but unintentional, detour – I got lost. When I finally got there, talks of the hot day expected were in earnest as well as the fact that those conditions called for less pressure in the tires than usual, otherwise the risk of getting a flat was very high. The message did not sink in at all, and I went ahead to the transition area to set up. I found some shade under a tree and started a game of back-and-forth to the restroom, repeating it about twenty times. I was a bit nervous.

The speaker at the event, Attila Péter, explained how difficult the hilly bike course was, and that it would truly separate those who could ride from the rest of the field. He reminded us to be sure to learn how to fix a flat before the race got under way, since that was a rudimentary skill for a triathlete. "Of course, it is." Truthfully, if I had ended up with a puncture, I wouldn't have known the first thing to do with my wheel. Nonetheless, to prepare for the worst, I watched a YouTube video on how to fix a flat (still in the comforting shade of the tree), which made it ever so clear that there was no way I would be able to fix one if I had to that day. "If I ever race in a triathlon again, then I will prove myself..."

Finally, the speaker brought up the topic of nutrition, energy bars and gels, and how to use them wisely and that it would be advisable to have one within an hour of the start. Having never tried anything like that before, not to mention that I had already lost a considerable amount of weight during the preceding hours, I wasn't going to take my chances – but, I thought, "next time, if there will actually be a next time, I will surely learn how to use those supplements after some experiments."

The time had come, and we were sent into the water without wetsuits. My lips turned purple very quickly; I was freezing. It

There Goes My Triathlon Virginity, the Night After a Wedding

only got worse after the start, because I saw nothing through my goggles, but a stirred up, muddy haze in which I was kicked and punched from every possible direction. Not the most therapeutic environment for one with hydrophobia – I was scared for my life within the first few minutes. While swimming, I made a decision – "If I get out of here alive, I will never go near a triathlon race again, that is for sure!" I wrestled through the freestyle, although I would have been much faster with my good old breaststroke. What can I say – I am stubborn like that.

It took me nearly 35 minutes to complete the 1500 meters, which put me in the notable 276th place out of the water. That is what I managed to put together in a field of 301 male participants, after three swim practices a week. In other words, I was feeling just a tad out of place. The speaker also gave me my due welcome as I entered the transition area when he exclaimed: *"And here comes the breaststroke crew...,"* and made his sensible remark of *"It is easy to find your bike now, since everyone has left already..."* I had to sit around for the good part of about four minutes before I finally came to my senses and was able to get geared up for the bike ride. "Now that I am here, there is no way I will give up this race, but the Ironman is surely out of the question."

With that, I was off, cracking those traditional pedals on my carefully selected, non-carbon Merida, to tackle the 40-kilometer (25 miles) bike course, which, to my great pleasure, was truly as hilly as forecasted. The funny thing is that I was actually happy about the difficult inclines because I just kept on passing my fellow competitors. It turned out that this course fell into the challenging category for most of them, but I had trained on very similar terrain on the road to Fót. It goes to show how much it matters what one is used to, since I could not compare my rides to anything else, this course seemed totally normal to me. As I gradually worked my way up into the middle of the field, I started to enjoy the race. I only got nervous when the lace of my running shoe got twisted around the pedal going up a hill and I felt that either I try to miraculously untangle while riding or I would surely crash and die zooming

Confessions of an Ironman

downhill. I managed to get it free. My lack of practice in cleaning my nasal passages was clearly visible on my gear by the end of the bike leg, and quite possibly on the others,' too. I completed the bike leg in 1 hour and 24 minutes and with huge relief that I didn't get a flat. The time caught me by surprise, since in training I had never gone that fast before.

I spent less than two minutes in the transition area where, with newfound spirits thanks to the great boost my "speedy" biking had given me, I started thinking that I might just do more triathlons after all, since all I had left was running, which I thought I was actually good at. I ran a 48-minute 10K, and although the last kilometers were very hard and I was really looking forward to the end, all in all, it went alright. I placed 125th among the men, with an overall time of 2 hours and 53 minutes. I felt pretty good about my time, considering the state I was in right after the swim and the number of people who were in front of me at that time.

My Velence adventure was a genuine emotional roller coaster. In under three hours' time, I went from the depths of *"I'll never do this again"* to the idea of *"I should sign up for a half Ironman."* Why not – I still had a few weeks to ride some more miles, and also enough time to test those energy bars. Not to mention, the finisher medals at those events say Ironman on them. Even if it's only a 70.3[7], in light of where I was only a few short months ago, that wouldn't be too bad at all.

---

[7] The 70.3-mile distance is half of a full Ironman, hence the name Ironman 70.3.

SIGHTS ON THE MEDAL THAT SAYS IRONMAN

The half Ironman I picked was scheduled for August 22, 2015. The distances were 1.2 miles of swimming followed by a 56-mile bike ride, and finally a half-marathon run (13.1 miles). The only thing I feared on that list was the biking. I put off signing up, as usual, and this time I had a rational reason; the conditions for cancellation were far from friendly and the fee was significantly higher than for other similar races. Up to that point, I had only been on a road bike 17 (!) times, and the farthest I had ridden at one time was 50 miles. I felt there was still much to be done, to say the least, and there were still quite a few hazy spots, such as the meaning of an SPD pedal or what an interval training session might include.

After the race in Velence, to everyone's delight, I returned to the bike store and declared I was ready for some SPD pedals, whatever they might be. After they were put on the bike, I got a flash tutorial and learned that from that point on, I would also be able to pull up on the pedals and not only press down, while riding with the proper bike shoes. I would surely discover how greatly beneficial that was, once I got used to it. *(To this day, I am still unsure how much of that benefit I was able to discover.)* In the meantime, they didn't beat around the bush and told me that first, before making the

Confessions of an Ironman

discovery, I would certainly experience a number of other things: "The first few times, you will surely forget to detach your shoe from the pedal and will fall over sideways. Do not worry though – everyone goes through that when they start, but still, be careful." After receiving the reassuring info packet, I chanted SPD, SPD all the way home. It only happened twice that I had to shuffle to keep my balance, almost falling on the cars that were next to me at the traffic lights, and managed to get home safely.

I was so pleased with the outcome of my shopping trip that I didn't even look at my bike for two weeks. My time was beginning to run out so I convinced myself that I had no reason riding any less than 56 miles – the distance of the bike leg of the 70.3 – once I did get back in the saddle. Finally, when I got out on the road, I extended my usual route, making the total elevation about 2300 feet, and managed to fight through the half Ironman bike distance in 3 hours and 37 minutes. It did not feel good at all. I was unhappy with both my time and the way I felt afterward, so I repeated the same 56-mile ride twice more in June. I detected no trace of improvement. Basically, I got to the point where I felt I could ride the distance if I had to, but I did not feel that I really wanted to do it.

I had to push hard in July for a realistic chance of being able to complete the race once I signed up for it. The only thing I had given up on before was the suicidal marathon preparation, when I lost my toenails and couldn't walk anymore; I was far from the prospect of giving up on this. On July 4, 2015, we went down to the lake crossing endurance swim again; this was my third one in a row. (The second one didn't bring about anything worth mentioning.) My plan was simple: "For the first time in my life, I want to swim 3.2 miles in freestyle, in open water, among other swimmers, no matter what it takes." That's what I thought was the most ideal way to prepare for the half Ironman, and the "no matter what it takes" aspect also came into play, as I was beginning to feel very sick in the car on our way there. I was fighting some sort of stomach virus complete with

Sights on the Medal that Says Ironman

throwing up and diarrhea, so it took me quite some time to gather myself and be able to start. What I remember is that it was very cold again and by the time I reached the 500-meter buoy I was already thinking that it was a very stupid idea, but was also adamant about making it to the opposite shore. I "washed up" on the other side after 2 hours and 25 minutes, which I could have done (and actually have done) faster even in breaststroke. Nevertheless, I did what I set out to do. I didn't have to wait long for Anikó to finish. I don't think I looked very sharp on the ferry ride back. A member of the medical crew started to shake me as I was peacefully sleeping, screaming that I was going to faint any second. No matter how hard I tried to convince her that I simply wanted to rest, she made me stay awake the rest of the way so that I wouldn't faint. Bravo to science! All in all, as far as I was concerned, the swimming dress rehearsal box had been ticked. Nothing would prevent me from completing a 1900-meter swim.

I made advancements on the running front, too. A couple of my teammates frequently mentioned during our morning bus rides to the pool that they also went to the club's running practices, and that I should check them out, too. I didn't really understand what good running loops on a track could do, especially over such short distances compared to what I usually ran, but I thought, what the heck, I'll give it a try. If memory serves me well, I ended up joining a session where we had to run 10 x 1000 meters. The target time for each kilometer was around four minutes, which gave us one minute or a bit less to rest before hitting the track again. Although I was able to do the set, I realized that the intensity and speed of my lonely creek runs were not even close. I thought perhaps I should add some interval sessions to my suicidal training plan. The way I understood it back then, real triathletes did 1000 meter repeats in five-minute intervals, which I could easily do on my own at the track near my house. Little did I know that interval trainings had infinite variations based on the desired training effect, and that these kinds of sessions should not be done back-to-back. Such an overload not only made it impossible to complete the increasingly

Confessions of an Ironman

difficult trainings I thought up for myself, but completely exhausted my body, too. Ultimately, I did a live experiment proving that all I later learned about sports science was well-founded and true.

From the Outside

The only reason I don't mind my usual "headfirst into the wall" approach in regard to running is that, thanks to it, I had one of the most intriguing experiences of my life at that neglected running track near my house. I once attended a presentation where Ferenc Szőnyi, a Hungarian ultra-triathlete, described how he experienced a sort of "out of body" sensation when he got dehydrated or his blood sugar levels dropped during demanding competitions. Based on the descriptions provided by Szőnyi, I am pretty sure I shared similar sensations when, right after a 10 x 1000 session the day before (!), I tackled a 15 x 1000 interval set in the scorching summer heat.

That was one of the most disastrous training sessions of my life. After only a few of those 1000 intervals, I was struggling to finish them under five minutes so that I could get going for the next one almost immediately, still with a skyrocketing heart rate. While I recognized that it was completely useless, since it was not an interval session anymore and I should just let it go, I was also devastated by my failure and my weakness.

The picture is still clear in my head to this day: For a split moment, I saw myself from above making my way around one of the bends of the track. I was able to tear myself out of the self-imposed guilt and all my feelings were put in a completely different light. "Am I feeling this bad simply because I cannot do four-minute 1000s today? Is this really the measure of my self-worth? What if I just accepted this as a fact, and still loved myself for who I am? And what if I expressed that love by allowing myself some rest?"

Sights on the Medal that Says Ironman

I stopped right there, jogged home, and lay down for a nap. I frequently recall this experience when something doesn't go quite as planned, which, in sports, happens all the time. Looking from a step back, all my struggles and worries seemed ridiculous. The extraordinary experience of seeing them from the outside made it possible for me not to take things so seriously, and to be able to accept what I could not change. This does not mean that now I just quit when things get tough. No, I'm still the kind of person who puts in all he has when in a group training session, but if things don't go as I previously imagined, they should not be fought against. By now, I have learned to accept that and know that I am still a good person, regardless of any given physical performance. This is a significant step forward when tackling an uncontrolled, compulsive urge to perform, which, in my opinion, so many of us have.

I made my decision about the half Ironman on June 11th, after a half-marathon distance night run where I averaged 7:27 minutes per mile. I wasn't taking any nutrition on board and yet I was still not fatigued at all. Naturally, I was pleasantly surprised and immediately drew the conclusion that I was in pretty good shape. I thought if I could somehow get through the bike portion, I should be able to complete the race with no problem.

Looking back at my training data, it is obvious I could have been much smarter with my bike preparation. For starters, I only went out to ride seven times in July. I rode 56 miles multiple times, but that distance still felt painfully long at the time, and I also put in a number of 30-milers immediately followed by a run. At the end of the month, I even ran a complete half-marathon after one of the 30-mile bike sessions. (According to the stats, I wasn't doing too bad because I didn't need more than 1 hour and 50 minutes for that run.) Altogether, I rode 317 miles in July, in the complete absence of any plan or the observation of the *gradual increase in workloads*

Confessions of an Ironman

theory. My Garmin recorded everything, but there was no coach yet who could have seen what I was doing – so there was no stopping me.

I saved my king ride for early August. Extending my usual route, I covered 68 miles with 2500 feet of elevation. I got completely drained. The adventure took me 4 hours and 13 minutes, during which not only was the heat torturing, but so was sitting in the saddle. My back, my neck, and basically every square inch of my body was in excruciating pain. I wasn't even in the vicinity of feeling that one day I could get used to this sport. I even questioned whether or not I wanted to get used to it. As for the full-distance Ironman bike leg, it was simply unfathomable to me – I simply could not see how a person could ride that far in one sitting.

With the date of the half Ironman slowly approaching, a morning bus ride brought a sharp turn in my preparation. Bálint, one of my teammates, told me that he did a lot of his bike rides on the tarmac ring around our national stadium. It was completely flat with no traffic to worry about, so he could practice maintaining the near 19 mph speed, which was about the minimum expectation. Needless to say, I could only meet that "minimum expectation" with the wind at my back or going downhill, but it was also true that I had never tried riding on flat terrain before. I liked the idea of a flat road without traffic, where I could ride at 19 mph until I fell off the bicycle. Truth is, I was also easily lured because Bálint said that the ring was just barely longer than one kilometer (0.6 miles), which would make long rides extremely boring there, so those sessions should still be done elsewhere.

Fired up by this new idea, I quickly forgot about my "mountainous" route around Fót. I was utterly bored with it by then, and only two days after my exhausting 68-mile adventure, I headed out to the tarmac ring. In the name of moderation, I cranked out 57 miles with an average speed of 18.4 mph. I was totally fine with having to repeat the same short loop over eighty times; I had time to think, I didn't have to worry about any vehicles running me over,

Sights on the Medal that Says Ironman

and I could completely focus on what I thought was important – namely, the speed and the distance at that point. (I did not own a heart rate monitor or a cadence meter.) As I recall, the beginning of the session felt easy, it was no problem keeping my speed above 19 mph. Later, leaving eating and drinking out of the equation, I got so spent that I had to keep standing out of the saddle and wrestle my way through a section of the loop each time in order to keep the expected splits. Being the practical man that I am, I was not satisfied with this attempt, as the 18.4 mph average speed I ended up with was slower than the "minimum expectation" that I had heard on the bus. Consequently, I sentenced myself to a quick redo. Someone had finally told me how fast I should ride on a flat course, which was more or less the description of the Budapest half Ironman bike course. I was slower than I needed to be, and the time I had left until the race was ticking away very quickly. (I had less than three weeks.)

I had one solution for such scenarios: "I press on, and keep training hard, regardless of how I feel, because there is not much time left to make up my deficit so that I can meet the minimum requirement." Consequently, two days later (!) I was on the tarmac loop again. I rode 57 miles and managed to squeeze out a 19 mph average. (You may notice that these bike sessions were in two-day successions, over distances of 68, 57, and again 57 miles, when even a single ride like that was enough to completely drain me. Not to mention, I knew nothing about nutrition, so I only carried water and perhaps an isotonic drink – but not a single energy bar or gel. It was a really bad way to train!) It was going to be a very hot day when I did the last ride, so I took off at 5:52 a.m. precisely, right after sunrise. When I got home, still before 9 a.m., our gardener looked at his watch in panic, thinking he must be late since I was already returning from a practice. We ended up exchanging a few words, but our really entertaining conversation came only after the race.

I completed four 56-mile bike sessions on the tarmac loop. I was the only lunatic around, so the gatekeeper recognized me after a while and greeted me from afar. Sometimes, I went for a 10K run right after

Confessions of an Ironman

the three-hour bike ride to see if I could still run following such an exhausting bicycle adventure. One of these stadium loop sessions was especially memorable because I managed to get a flat riding around and around. By then, I owned the proper tools to change an inner tube, and I had even tried it out at home, in the comfort of my living room, recruiting a little help from YouTube. That morning, though, I was far from my "controlled lab environment" and was forced to solve the problem on a patch of grass by the tarmac ring, in the growing heat of the rising summer sun. It was not a short pit stop, for sure! At times I honestly thought my bike would never have a rear wheel again, but eventually I managed to get the job done and completed what remained of my self-prescribed training session. Let me just say that my performance did not convince me that I would be able to handle a similar problem during a race.

IF THAT IS HOW ONE SHOULD RIDE A BIKE, THEN I DON'T KNOW WHAT I'M DOING!

The official bike course preview for the Budapest half Ironman was on August 15th, early in the morning. I wanted to be there for it because, in all honesty, even that preview, let alone the race, made me very nervous. The course preview troubled me in a number of ways. For one, I had to ride across Budapest to get to the race center. Up until that point, I had always tried to stay away from traffic. I always picked the shortest route to get out of the city when I hit the road toward Fót, and the stadium loop was less than two miles from my house. Navigating a "metropolitan city-jungle ride" was way outside my comfort zone. Furthermore, I knew that the 56-mile race course was comprised of two loops, which meant that the athletes, previewing the course in a pack, were to ride about 28 miles. It wasn't the distance that worried me, it was the idea of a "pack" that made me restless. I had always ridden alone and having never seen other riders around me, I was in for quite a surprise a week before the race.

Sights on the Medal that Says Ironman

We averaged a tad under 19 mph for the course preview and I was happy to see that the total elevation in the loop was only about 330 feet – it was nothing compared to my Fót training course. What caught me by great surprise, though, was how the others pedaled when on the test loop (and most probably at all other times, too). I had never seen anything like it.

Keeping a 19 mph speed seemed effortless for them. Everyone was set on easy gears, which meant that while my cranks went around once, the others' did 2-3 revolutions. I was still living in the world of "tough gears for tough guys." My approach was rooted in the way I perceived triathlon training: It is a tough sport, so I turned the highest gears when riding. Since no one told me that this was nonsense, I simply took it for granted that we turn hard gears on the flats and only ease up on the more difficult inclines. The others must have thought differently; they put very little effort into keeping a speed which was quite painful for me to maintain after some time.

It was only later that I learned that pedaling cadence was an important factor in biking, and that it was possible to go over 19 mph in lower gears, too, with my legs spinning faster. My awakening was kindled when I saw what my professional training plan listed for the first week, which I was given for my full-distance Ironman preparation. When I started asking questions, my coach laughed so hard that I practically knocked his wind out. We had a lot of fun with that – but let's not jump ahead.

I did not change anything in my biking strategy after the group ride. It was quite simple – I would turn the hardest gears all the way through, except when the course turned up into the Buda Castle. That hill was steep enough to allow for a little easing up.

RACE WEEK AT THE PEAK OF EXHAUSTION

As part of my brilliant "homemade" training plan, I put in a 10K run right after a nearly 19-mile bike ride in the first half of the

Confessions of an Ironman

race week. I followed this with a shortened 12-mile + 10K combo on Wednesday. By then, I had tapped my energy levels dry with mindless training sessions which lacked even the slightest shred of sensible thought or expertise. I didn't have the faintest idea as to what should be done in the final days before the race.

Competitors were allowed to test the water in the bay, where the swimming was going to take place, on August 20th. I was especially interested as I had never tried the wetsuit I bought before the race in Velence, where (according to the organizers) the water was too warm, so they did not allow it. The "dress rehearsal," similarly to all my previous open water endeavors, was not a very pleasant experience. Thanks to one of my experienced teammates, however, I got a chance that afternoon to learn how to put on a wetsuit properly. I was informed that, if I do it right, I would not even have to worry about using Vaseline to prevent chafing. This was good news since I didn't have any on me. (There it was, finally, the answer to the Vaseline question! Years before, when brought up jokingly in a chat with a friend, the subject had been quite funny indeed. Now, in my pre-race state of mind, I did not find it amusing at all.)

I was not nervous about the race – I was petrified by it. Fresh off my panicky swim in Velence, I was scared of the first discipline, too, even though I didn't see the distance as challenging due to my three swim sessions a week. As for the bike, my greatest fear was getting a flat, which I might or might not be able to fix. The course, compared to the "Fót Mountains" seemed easily doable, and I was convinced that if I managed to take it home with the bike, there was nothing that could prevent me from finishing a half-marathon, no matter what state I was in. (I was almost proven wrong about the latter.)

For a final challenge, I rode to the race center across town to check in my bike, and to make sure I knew what, where, and in what order I would need to do when I come out of the water. I ate what they gave me at the pre-race pasta party and I returned home while juggling the following thoughts: "I want to complete the bike leg under 3 hours on that flat course. The half-marathon could not take longer than 2 hours, even in a near-death state. Including the unpredictable swim and transition times, I should be able to finish under 6 hours. The only thing that could stand in my way is a technical problem on the bike; all else will be up to me."

Fear is Natural – Learn to Use it!

There will always be fear. Even the best athletes admit that they are afraid, just like the amateurs. There is one significant thing they do differently, though: They do not fight it, they use it to their advantage.

My favorite boxer, Mike Tyson, wrote in his autobiography that Cus D'Amato, his very first, childhood coach, once told him: "What's the difference between the hero and the coward? There ain't no difference. They both feel exactly the same on the inside: They both fear dying and getting hurt. It's what the hero does that makes him a hero. And what the other doesn't do, makes him a coward."

Fear can only control you until you try to fight it, feeding it with your anxious energy. From the moment you simply accept its presence and stop trying to make it go away, you can begin to dance with it, using its energy to help you move forward in the right direction. It is like aikido, a traditional Japanese martial art. The essence of the techniques is that one uses the opponent's energy to execute each move. Tony Robbins used this analogy, too. I also found many great points in the book entitled *Feel the Fear and Do It Anyway*[8] on how to treat fear, as it is something that we cannot make disappear as long as we live.

---

[8] Susan Jeffers: *Feel the Fear and Do It Anyway.*

THE MORNING HAS COME! "ARE YOU GOING TO WEAR THAT BLANKET FOR THE SWIM?"

I was so scared I could hardly sleep. I wrote down a few things about my experience after the race was over and it says that I was wide awake after one in the morning and had such a bad case of diarrhea that I lost a significant amount of weight. I could not have been in worse shape on race morning, not to mention that those who actually slept woke up to unusually cold weather.

We quickly got ready, and after forcing down the usual minimalistic scrambled egg breakfast, we were on our way to the race center. It was cold enough to make standing around wearing nothing but a race singlet very uncomfortable, so I wrapped myself in an IKEA blanket. In the middle of that huge crowd, I turned inward to be alone with my thoughts. "If I finish, I will get a medal with the Ironman logo on it. I don't belong here at all. I don't want to finish last!" One of those innate fears which Tony Robbins taught us about in London clearly emerged from my thoughts, echoing the notion, "I am not good enough." I lost track of time while all those thoughts were bouncing around in my head. The next thing I remember is the announcement letting us know that we could enter the water for warmup, which I didn't even want to get near until I absolutely, positively had to. My wonderment ended when one of my teammates looked over and kindly asked, "Are you going to wear that blanket for the swim? Don't you want to put on your wetsuit instead?"

This brought me back to reality and while I started cursing myself for undertaking such a huge challenge, I also knew there was no turning back. I began to get geared up and slowly approached the water when our age group was called to the start.

We had a few minutes to get situated. Most people continued to swim, but I kept to the beach, waiting for the start signal which was a cannon fire. It seemed incomprehensible what I had gotten myself into; the mere thought of putting my feet in the water was

Sights on the Medal that Says Ironman

hard to imagine in that piercing cold. I only had minutes until the start, so I had to dig deep and pull out the goal realization recipe which had worked for me so many times before. At that point, there was nowhere to hide. I had to run the race, there was no plan B. "Let's take it one by one! I have gained the knowledge necessary to reach my goal, I am good enough in all three disciplines to be able to complete the required distances. This makes the first step a check, so we can move onto the next one. Let's break down this enormous and seemingly unattainable task lying in front of us into steps." There were only seconds to the start signal, so I had no time for overthinking: "As a first step, I'll enter the water with the others here in the back, and I will make my way to the buoy that is about 10 yards out in front of us. The rest, I will figure out while I am swimming. The third component of the success recipe is perfectly captured in the Nike slogan: "Just do it!" The cannon went off, I waved to Anikó, and I slowly started walking toward the water. My adventure was under way.

IRONMAN 70.3 BUDAPEST: A SERIES OF SURPRISES

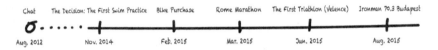

I definitely considered myself to be a weak swimmer. After my catastrophic struggles during the Velence race, my plan was to begin the first discipline from the back of my start wave, yielding to the real swimmers. That way, I thought, I might be able to avoid getting kicked around, and could swim in relatively calm waters. I was among the very last ones walking into the water. I didn't skip or run like many of the other, seemingly more professional competitors.

Fortunately, the buoys were placed in very close proximity, so I did not wander much off the swim course. I felt strong enough in the water, despite being so depleted from overtraining, but I couldn't have guessed my position in the field. I was convinced I was somewhere at the end of the group I took off with, since I was awfully slow. As I couldn't really see much in the water, which was far from crystal clear, I had no idea how many people might have been in front of or behind me. I only realized that I was actually passing people who wore different colored caps from ours when I turned onto the "finishing" stretch of the swim course. Those caps had started a few minutes before us, so I was thinking either our entire group had passed them, or I am not dead last. When I looked at my watch, coming out of the water, I saw that I finished the 1900-meter swim under 38 and a half minutes, which totally exceeded my expectations. As an added bonus, I wasn't scared for my life, and finished 116th out of 207 athletes in my age group. Naturally, I didn't have this information right out of the water, so as I was struggling to make it look like I was running to the transition area, I glanced over my shoulder and was very happy to note that I hadn't ended up last in my weakest discipline.

In hindsight, I should have taken the swim a lot easier, which was evidenced by my lack of coordination as I arrived at the transition area. I was still disoriented even after I changed for the bike ride. I was so out of it that I completely missed my bike and ran past it. Someone I had had a chat with while setting up the day before shouted out and asked, "Aren't you parked that way?" I thanked him and turned right around. So much for a professional transition.

Up next – the bike ride! I had two constant worries about the bike: One was getting a flat and the other was getting rained on – with a very good chance for the latter that day. I had never ridden on wet roads before, but I was told that rain could make things surprisingly tricky, and since I already had enough to worry about just getting in the saddle, I really could have done without the added stress. In response to my twofold fear, I rode faster than ever, trying to escape from both the flat and the rain, while turning the highest gear possible, of course. I hit a 22 mph pace to start. Obviously, I could not maintain it, not to mention that, despite all the advice I was given, I only took one bottle of isotonic drink and a single energy bar for the whole ride. I got completely spent on the bike. Partly, because I got carried away and went much harder than what I was prepared for, and also because I turned way too tough gears. These mistakes, and the complete lack of a thought-through nutrition plan, could not have led to anything but emptying my gas tanks painfully early in the race.

Nonetheless, I was determined to finish, no matter what – unless, of course, the bike fell into pieces under me. I became more and more fatigued and started to count down the remaining road, five kilometers at a time (every three miles), using the distance markers

Confessions of an Ironman

I passed. I remember that it was around mile 44 when the feeling that I was actually going to make it started to get stronger. There was 4, 3, 2, and then finally 1 last 3-mile section I had to cover without a puncture. My bike held out just fine, and, by the time I started the run, the threat of rain had passed and the day got quite sunny and warm.

I was totally wiped out by the end of the bike leg and couldn't really keep the 19 mph speed anymore. Thanks to my efforts in the beginning, I had built up enough cushion to end with a 2-hour and 50-minute overall time for the 56-mile ride. I had beaten my goal of 3 hours. As I was changing in the transition area, it was evident that I was far from the optimal state to start the run, but my "childhood-frustration-compensating medal-collecting motivation" was stronger. "Just one more half-marathon, and I will have an Ironman finisher medal. The danger of any mechanical problems that could potentially stop me is gone, there is no machine to depend on now, only myself, and I will not stop until I finish."

That was the mindset I started the 13.1 mile run with and, as usual, I went out too fast. I generally struggle keeping myself in check right after biking and have difficulty settling into a running pace I can reliably maintain over the given distance. I was still so inexperienced, and also so overly enthusiastic, that I didn't even think of what I was doing. The near 7-minute per mile pace with which I hit the course was overly ambitious for my fitness level at the time.

We had to run four laps and for the first two, I had no major issues. On the third one, though, I started clocking over 9:40-minute miles, which was a huge shift to the other end of the spectrum for me. "I never run this slow!" Going into it as the inexperienced "athlete" that I was, I did not factor in that, by then, I had been racing for over five hours straight, and my solution for refueling was a single energy bar and a little isotonic drink during the bike ride. As it turned out, my nutrition plan was less than satisfactory, which became crystal clear when, around mile 9, I thought I was going to pass out. Up to that point, because of my previous night's perpetual bathroom visits with diarrhea, I hadn't used the closely-placed aid stations for more than to help keep up my good spirits while getting cheered on, and to exchange a few words. Then, however, I knew I had arrived at a point where I had to throw caution into the wind and consume something that I had never tried before. It didn't really make a difference anymore how I was going to destroy the race I had managed to put together up until that point – either by shocking my system with something it could not take in and ending up in a mobile toilet, or by bonking and not being able to carry on because of complete exhaustion. Either way, the day would surely end in disaster.

I had nothing to lose, so Powerbar or Coke, it didn't matter what it was. I devoured and gulped down everything I could get my hands on at each aid station. Having zero knowledge as to what a nutrition plan should look like, and with my spirits six feet under because of my diminished running pace, I didn't think twice about anything at that point. The effects came fairly quickly: My pace increased by about 20 seconds per mile, and my mood started to climb out of the hole to make me look fairly collected for the last lap, where I ran well inside the 9:40 per mile pace. I was even able to accelerate in the final stretch before crossing the finish line.

Only Anikó had accompanied me to the race. Before I began my last lap, one of my good friends showed up by her side, which made me very happy. "I can't let him see me crawling! There it is – one more reason to get myself together." Just before I finished, a few yards out from the line, I spotted my family, too. They had come from out of town and made it there just in the nick of time.

To finish the Budapest 70.3, I ran a 1-hour and 48-minute half-marathon, which, to this day, seemed to be the longest one of my life. When I crossed the finish line and glanced at my watch, the race time read 5 hours and 25 minutes. I was way inside my 6-hour goal, but before I could begin to soak that in, I found myself receiving a commending handshake from the race organizer, and that certain medal with the Ironman logo was hung around my neck. The

Confessions of an Ironman

earning of the medal had seemed simply unthinkable just a few short months before.

I found myself a spot in the finishers' area and, with a fruit beer in my hand that the hostess had given me, I collapsed onto the grass. I kept looking at my medal and my finishing time. I was very happy but my emotions were also mixed. I felt a victim, because I had forced myself to undertake that far-from-normal preparation to be able to squeeze out that result. Crossing the finish line was (or rather should have been) my deliverance. On the other hand, I was truly proud, because my result was way beyond anything I could have imagined. That was it, I collected myself, I picked up my beautiful finisher T-shirt, snapped some pictures with the family, and then consumed enough food in the athletes' tent to feed a normal person for a few days. (Fortunately, I have never had to worry about my weight. Later, when I was following a more serious training regimen, and I regularly consumed as much in one sitting as a whole family would in a day, my eating habits called for some attention, though.)

One Oil Barrel at a Time

I once read a story by Brian Tracy, a best-selling author and motivational speaker, where he talked about how he drove across the Sahara Desert. The roughly 500-mile road was marked with unused, black oil barrels. The barrels were placed about 3 miles apart so, in daylight, only two of them were visible at a time: One, which was just passed and another that was up ahead. The task was simple – reach the next barrel, keeping it in sight while driving toward it. That way, it ensured you were going in the right direction. That is how he crossed the world's largest and most dangerous desert, and that is exactly how all truly big goals are reached.

The goal has to be broken down into smaller parts, all the while keeping your focus only on the next step. A goal can be

Ironman 70.3 Budapest: A Series of Surprises

overwhelming in its entirety. Sometimes it can be difficult to wrap your mind around everything that needs to be done, and those thoughts could easily lead to quitting.

I didn't even want to do the Budapest 70.3 race. Standing there on the shore, wrapped in that blanket, I viewed the first buoy as the first oil barrel. It was beyond any question that I could get myself that far. On the bike, I counted down the remaining road ahead by three-mile stretches; I focused on one three-mile segment at a time which was to be conquered at the required pace, rendering each of the steps doable, as I cut the distance slowly down to nothing.

Finally, on the run, the colored bracelets we received every time we began a new lap also helped. That's how the organizers knew where everyone was in the race. All that had to be done was to collect the next color. If you focused on the next, seemingly feasible step, you would eventually arrive at the big result.

I was told later that when my little brother Bence, who was six at the time, heard that I crossed the finish line, his response was: "Thank God he came out alive." As it turned out, some sort of TV coverage also aired about the race. The gardener, whom I had frightened in the early morning some time before, stopped me a few days later to tell me how big a sports fan he was and that he saw me on TV doing this "Iron Maiden thing." It was pretty funny.

Ultimately, I was happy with my very first half Ironman performance. I began to understand what everyone meant by telling me that I was going to learn a lot about myself by the time I could become an Ironman finisher. My feeling was that even the half distance opened the door to some profound realizations in connection with the "I am not good enough" feelings and all of their side effects. I was filled with both curiosity and fear as I wondered what there could be for me in the second act – if there was going to be one at all.

IS THIS IT? OR IS THIS ONLY HALF THE JOURNEY? I'LL RUN THIS HOME COURT MARATHON, AND THEN I'LL THINK IT OVER

I am predominantly a cerebral man. I think and calculate all the time, and after the half-distance race, I had a lot to ponder. Self-reflection, where you are able to look at yourself from the outside, analyzing your own thoughts and feelings, is a wonderful thing because it can bring about highly valuable realizations. For example, I knew that if the race I had just completed was the real Ironman – meaning that the classic distance consisted of 1.2 miles swimming, 56 miles biking, and 13.1 miles of running, then I would have been done. There would have been nothing to push me further and strive to do a triathlon that was twice as long, since I "simply" wanted to be an Ironman. I wasn't interested in doing a double, triple, or any other special-distance event at all.

This is very curious, because if you think about it, it means I realized that all I really needed was the Ironman title, a means to a sort of self-validation. (The reason why, I wasn't yet ready to see, or rather to have the courage to see.) With that said, it was never really a question of what I actually had to do in order to earn that title.

Is This It? Or Is This Only Half the Journey?

It could very well have been jumping through flaming hoops on horseback over endless miles; I would do what needed to be done because I just had to become an Ironman. What I had just done was not that. It was the half distance, and half things have never satisfied me. I don't run half-marathons, I don't order half a beer in a pub. Although I did make a feeble attempt to find a way to make my achievement satisfying, especially so I would not have to carry on torturing myself with the preparations for the full distance, I wasn't really confident in my ability to not see the shiny Ironman logo on my medal as a symbol of my surrender halfway to the goal. Instead of making me proud, I knew this would eventually upset me each time I looked at it. "If I fold now and don't finish what I have started..."

Nevertheless, I allowed myself some time and a chance for my brain to accept the possibility that the 70.3 race was an achievement sufficient enough to prove whatever needed to be proven and make me believe that I was done. I would have been happy with that script. All the more so, because I had no idea what to do next. This race made it clear to me that I had reached the best possible performance I was capable of with such brainless preparation and lacking any background knowledge. Completing the full distance still seemed out of reach. I simply could not wrap my head around it. "That takes much more strength and a completely different preparation, which I just cannot do alone. I need help – if that's what I really want."

I have rather strange notions about rest, or how to reassess my goals, and also about post-race recovery in general. Weeks before the Budapest 70.3, it caught my attention that there was a marathon in my hometown on the 30th of August, one week after the half Ironman. A couple of things kept me thinking about it: I could run at home, so even my little brother from my father's side, who was six at the time, could be out on the course cheering for me. I also loved the finisher medal.

Confessions of an Ironman

I hadn't signed up for it before the triathlon and I even told Anikó, right after I finished in Budapest, that there was no way I could run a marathon within a week in Jászberény. I gave myself a day's rest after the 70.3 on Sunday, which I declared to be my well-deserved recovery time, but on Monday I was already out on my track doing a 10x1000-meter session, alone, running at a 6:50 to 7 minutes per mile pace. On top of that, just in case that wouldn't suffice, on Tuesday (the very next day!) I went for a 15x1000, which was followed by an 8-miler at the creek, and I went for an even shorter jog on Thursday! It was absolutely insane, but I had no coach who could have told me to stop. When I was training with the team, I never told anyone about my marathon adventures; nobody asked, and neither did I feel inclined to talk about it.

With all that under my belt, I set off for Jászberény on the 30th of August to run the marathon. We happened to be in the middle of a merciless heatwave, for which even the authorities had issued a warning. My plan was to go easy, making it a kind of pleasure run, merely for the fun of it, and collect the medal. I was strong enough, or so I thought, and if I could just take it lightly and not get carried away, I might even enjoy it. Contrary to how I initially saw it, being home didn't exactly make things easier for me. On the way to the start, a heatwave warning of the highest level was mentioned on the car radio, advising people to stay inside if at all possible. My mom wasn't exactly on cloud nine knowing I was about to run a marathon instead of staying indoors in a cool room.

Framing Does Matter

How you perceive things makes an enormous difference. It could be "just" warm or there could be a red HEATWAVE WARNING sign flashing in front of your eyes. If the temperature is still about 97-100 degrees, your perception affects how you handle the situation.

> I have always tried my best to avoid anyone who labeled the things that I was about to do as "painfully difficult" or "impossible." If I am not told that something is impossible, I can do it! Albert Einstein hit the nail on the head when he said, "Everyone knew it was impossible, until a fool who didn't know came along and did it."
>
> It is important to understand that the spoken word has immense power and to use that to your advantage!

ME? TO THE PODIUM? ARE YOU SURE?

I think it was about 100 degrees when the 11 a.m. start rolled around. The heat was brutal, and I wasn't what you'd call rested, to say the least. I decided to go for an 8 minute per mile pace, which I thought would get me through the majority of the distance. I was wrong. According to my watch, my 9th mile was already way outside that tempo. I then did something I had not been known to do: I did not fight it. Even though I did try to get near the tempo I imagined would work, when I still couldn't quite do it, it did not bother me at all.

My heat management strategy consisted of drinking some water at each aid station, which were placed about 1 to 2 miles apart, and also dumping a few cups of water on myself. It was a two-lap course, and for a short section of each lap, we had to run on a nicely shaded forest trail. It was pretty crowded in the first lap, but as we got back to where we started from and began the second lap, I noticed that there wouldn't be much pushing and shoving, as many runners had decided to cut the distance in half due to the extreme conditions, and instead of continuing the torture, they went for the gulyas soup and beer the organizers had provided for the participants.

I started the second half of the marathon with a fairly good 8:50 per mile pace. At the end of the forest trail section, members of my enthusiastic fan club – my 6-year-old and 28-year-old brothers

Confessions of an Ironman

– even ran with me for a few hundred yards. Bence, the younger of the two, could hardly breathe, the poor guy, so that much running was plenty enough for him. Actually, I was more worried about him over that short bit of road than about myself over the whole race. I passed quite a few people in the forest, some of whom shouted, cheering me on. I didn't think much of it as I had no clue how many of us were still out there or where I was in the field of runners. Conscious racing is not my strong suit.

I got really scared, after leaving my eager supporters behind, when I saw people lying on the pavement and the medical team was pushing air into their mouths with a respiratory pump. The conditions were nothing short of extreme, so it was a smart decision to take the race relatively easy and to drink and "shower" at each aid station. Seeing all those victims convinced me that it was much better to run a mile outside 9:40 here and there than lying on the ground with them. I switched to an even slower pace. Being preoccupied with all that, it didn't even bother me that I went off course at one time, and it took the volunteer girls from the aid station I had just passed quite some time to shout after me that I needed to run the other way.

So few of us remained for the second lap that the fans, who popped up here and there by the course where it was winding through town, treated everyone as if they were heroes. There were girls who screamed – which is always nice – and we also came across the usual "running experts," one of whom remarked as I went past him, "Now, that is the perfect running build – easy for you." Since a marathon can be quite monotonous, I had plenty of time on my hands to think about that. Is it really about the physical build? Out on my home course, on the banks of Rákos Creek, the runners I always admired were those who got out there and did all they could for their health, despite their considerable excess weight. It is commendable when people for whom even a few hundred yards can be highly challenging tackle it, and instead of giving up, they value each small step as they progress, finding strength in every little triumph, even if it is just running their very first mile without stopping and carrying on from there. In my view (on the

Is This It? Or Is This Only Half the Journey?

recreational level) the question of build is secondary. Those who are willing to put in the necessary work and persevere, will sooner or later become successful. The others will always manage to find external factors that they can blame and use as an excuse not to exert considerable efforts. "Now, that is the perfect running build – easy for you."

I had failed to remind my overly excited little brother (or rather my father) that following me along the course in the car while waiving and cheering might not be the best idea, as it could easily mess with my rhythm. Despite this challenge, and perhaps due to my extreme caution with my pace, my thoughts were perpetually occupied with the quest on: "When will I hit the wall from where all I will be able to rely on to finish is my will power? I'm going to get there around mile 19, I am sure." When the wall didn't come, I put my next confident bet on mile 22 – and when I did not sense considerable fatigue at mile 25 either, I thought, "What the heck, I am gonna put a bit more into what is left."

Thanks to my acceleration, I was exhausted by the time I crossed the finish line and clocked a 3-hour 44-minute time, which was way off my personal best (my 3-hour 36-minute time in Rome). On the other hand, it had no significance for me whatsoever. My family commented that at the finish I was walking around as if I had done nothing, while the man who came in a few minutes earlier was getting an IV from the medical crew, being on the verge of fainting. Fortunately, I was fine. After receiving my medal, I was ready to go and get something to eat, or would have been if one of the organizers hadn't grabbed me and taken me to the monitor at the finish line. He pointed at my name and asked if that was me, because if it was, he said, I should stick around and wait until the awards ceremony. I took third place in the not-so-populated field of my age group. That sort of accident had never happened to me – and I suspect, won't happen very often in the future, either. I thoroughly enjoyed the situation. (Unlike some of my family members who saw this as more of a burden; it meant that they were forced to stay out in the heat for a few more hours because of me.)

Confessions of an Ironman

It was very exciting to be called onto the podium, where I received a small trophy and a bottle of white wine. The latter, besides a commending handshake, was accompanied by a classic Jászberény thought, which made me feel right at home: "It's alright, but not one for culinary pleasures."

TWO DAYS, TWO TALKS, AND A DECISION TAKING SHAPE

After my success in Jászberény, I gave myself a week's rest. I did the usual three swim practices, but didn't run at all. As for the bike, I had long forgotten about that since the half- distance race, and getting back on it hadn't even crossed my mind.

While I had been busy getting ready for the 70.3 race, someone I knew had completed the full Ironman in Nagyatád. That was *the* Ironman in Hungary, so I invited him for a cold one so he could tell me all about his experience and perhaps give me some advice. Naturally, I would not have missed asking him my favorite question for the world: "What would you do differently?"

Gábor and I initially met at a type of personal development training where we found ourselves in an interesting situation. We had to write down a goal that we wanted to accomplish yet were afraid of at the same time. Once done, we had to read what was on our papers to the person sitting next to us, and vice versa. We hadn't met before. When the trainer signaled, he was the one to start. He turned to me and said that he wanted to do an Ironman race. My paper read the same thing – it was shocking, to say the least.

I had been nowhere with my training then, far from even the marathon. I was still in a sort of dreaming phase, fantasizing that one day I might be able to do something like that. Gábor was way

Confessions of an Ironman

ahead of me – at least as far as running was concerned. We tagged each other on Facebook and basically that was it, but this small point of connection enabled me to see what sporting events he did and when, and how he was marching toward his goal. It was motivating and also extremely helpful in critical situations because it evoked the feeling that "Hey, I have already declared my commitment to the completion of an Ironman, even if it was to a stranger. There is no turning back from here – I have said it out loud, so I must do it."

Integrity as the Foundation of Success

Integrity simply means that you live in accordance with your deepest values. You are honest, and you keep your word. It is the harmony of thought, speech, and action.

As simple and natural as this may sound, too few live with integrity nowadays. Unfortunately, the dissolution of integrity can lead to profound inner conflicts in an individual. Many people are afraid to speak their minds and, while hiding their own thoughts from even themselves, they try to live up to expectations imposed by their environment. Even though their inner compass, which is aligned with their values, is pointing in the right direction, they override their own thoughts and feelings. As a result, their speech does not reflect them.

In my opinion, the dissolution of the harmony of thought and speech described above "only" results in an inner conflict in the beginning. On the next level, when a person's actions are not in line with what they say anymore, the result has much more immediate, external impacts as well. Such a person can quickly be regarded as undependable and as someone who should not be taken seriously.

The best approach is to make your words one with your thoughts and actions. Life can become much simpler if you can put aside the manipulative games and the compulsions to

> conform to external expectations, not to mention how much better that can make you feel. It was no surprise that I worried many people in my immediate circle when I first said I wanted to do an Ironman. They knew that it was going to happen, and the only question was when.
>
> It would make all aspects of our lives better if people rediscovered their innate integrity. That would make it possible for us to trust what the majority of people said at face value and not limit that circle of trust to a smaller group of exceptions.

By 2015, Gábor had reached a level where he could sign up for the Ironman in Nagyatád. He successfully completed it, fulfilling the dream he had written down and read to me many years before. Meeting him for a beer and to talk seemed like a good idea. It turned out, I was right.

Listening to his story, the feeling that I wanted to live through something like that, too, became stronger and stronger in me. On top of that, he told me that the time I had put into my preparations for the Budapest half Ironman was a whole lot more than what he had been able to devote to his training preparing for the full distance. He thought I had no reason to wait and should sign up for the race in 2016. I also liked Gábor's attitude because he didn't care about the pitying reactions he received when people around him learned what his final time for the race had been (13 hours and 53 minutes), and how sorry they were that this was all he could manage. He saw it in a completely different light. He had done something that only a minuscule fraction of the country would have been able to, and he was very proud of himself. He also affirmed what Dani had told me: Once he crossed the finish line, he didn't feel that he would ever have to put anything more or better on the table. It was perfect just the way it was. I had never been fully satisfied with anything I had done up to that point, and a feeling of pride had never entered my life – despite the fact that, realistically, I had plenty to be proud

Confessions of an Ironman

of. Hearing that the Ironman had given someone just what I was longing to experience gave me added motivation. I cannot say that I made up my mind then and there to enter the race, but it certainly got me closer to the decision.

The very next day I met with another friend, Márk, who had been working in the field of PR communication in a fairly high position for a long time. He had been interested in spirituality for some time and was becoming more and more serious about it as time went on. Our talk was quite a bit different from the one I had with Gábor, but it was in the course of the conversation when I first realized – and said out loud – that my Ironman project was the product of my uncontrolled performance compulsion, propelled by my "I am not good enough" and "I am weak" feelings. However, recognizing this, I opened the door to be able to work on them consciously, and make some changes. I also asserted – hastily, I must add – that my adventure was more a path to self-realization by then, and not a longing to conform to external expectations. Truth is, that was still far from reality. Later, during difficult training periods, I often caught myself sinking back into the role of the self-punishing victim who feels deeply sorry for himself because of the various tortures he must endure, or better yet, is forced to voluntarily undertake. It took me a very long time before I was capable of changing that, which was only possible by practicing self-reflection, looking at what I was doing from an outside vantage point, nipping my faulty thoughts in the bud, and not letting them roam freely to distort my feelings and, as a result, the quality of my life.

Besides recognizing the importance of self-realization, I was also able to admit that the whole project would only make sense if I was able to see my own success in it, if I could focus on my own achievement without comparing myself to anyone else. This liberating view was fundamental to being able to make my preparation as effective as it could be, from the standpoint of both performance and life experience.

I had read it in countless books and heard it in numerous seminars: The only sensible comparison is my own self from yesterday to today. My brain was aware of this, but I was unable to fully live by that reality. Any other comparison, besides being completely pointless, could easily become outright harmful. Obviously, this is not the case among competitive athletes, but my Ironman was only about me, about crossing my own boundaries, about proving something to myself which could liberate me from a long list of self-limiting beliefs. That is what would make it all worthwhile. I would not be setting world records anyway.

Booked-up Therapists

These harmful but also quite common comparisons of ourselves to others do not only exist in hobby sports. If you spend some time scrolling through Facebook, it is more than likely you'll find that the majority of people you see have arranged quite an impressive display of themselves: Trips to exotic places, great family times, cute pets, amazing food, etc. It generates a lot of frustration in many people when they come across these posts, especially if they happen to be living through a less-than-favorable phase of their own lives. It is inevitable that many come to the conclusion that "others are doing so well while I am in this rot." Looking beyond those shiny Facebook posts, however, we find that therapists are constantly snowed under, which goes to show that something is not quite right in "wonderland." Chances are you'll bump into the person you envied on Facebook today in a therapist's waiting room tomorrow, assuming you are both brave enough to face your problems.

It was during the event with Tony Robbins when I first thought I might need to focus on something entirely different than pretentious happiness to ensure that my life was headed

Confessions of an Ironman

in the right direction, regardless of what anyone else does. In order to make that happen, all I had to do was recognize my negative beliefs *(I am not good enough; I am not masculine enough)* and change them to more constructive ones *(I am a strong man)*. Obviously, it is not as simple as it sounds! To illustrate this, Tony asked us to picture our positive belief as a tabletop. All tabletops need legs to stand on. Consequently, we need to gather the "legs," or reasons, to support our new belief, which would help us accept its trueness.

Naturally, I had plenty to put on my list from my life experiences, but I still felt that if one of those legs under my new tabletop was an Ironman completion, that would certainly reinforce my belief that I was strong, I was good enough, and I could really do anything I set my mind to. Clearly, the Ironman is not the only thing one could do to prove that to himself, nonetheless, those were my thoughts at the time.

Truth is, at that point, my decision had been made. I didn't yet have the courage to admit it, even to myself. To be able to put it into words and to take the next step – which proved to be the most important one in realizing my goal – I needed a profound, external impact, a shock of some sort.

THIS IS NOT GOING TO WORK!
I NEED HELP!

For a final challenge in 2015, I wanted to complete the Budapest Marathon. The event was being held on October 11th and my plan was to break my personal best of 3 hours and 36 minutes. I dove into the preparations, sticking to my usual ways.

In light of what you have read thus far, "*my usual ways*" do not mean with a whole lot of success. I was completely drained, having taken no time to rest the entire year. I began my solitary training the second week of September, including the 1000 meter repeats at my home track (the way I saw it, real triathletes do "1000s" – a wisdom I based on the one and only team practice I had joined up until then.) I also completed several over 13 mile long runs by the creek. All that, in and of itself, wouldn't seem interesting enough to write about had I not been forced into a disgraceful surrender of my training plan, or rather, into a total retailoring of it, after only one short week. The event occurred on September 14th.

I prescribed myself the usual "treatment," so there was nothing new: 10x1000 meters in five-minute intervals. This meant that I was to run each 1000 well under five minutes so as to give myself some time to rest in between. Generally, that had not been a problem. On that day, right around the sixth "act." I slowed down so drastically that I barely made it in under the five minute mark. By my eighth attempt, it took me 5 minutes 23 seconds to run a 1000, even though

I put all I had into it. My mind was racing during the entire running session. First, I was utterly disappointed with myself – I just could not accept that I was not capable of more. My destructive thoughts were so deeply distressing that as I was doing my loops, I came to a point where I had a flash image, as if I were looking at myself from outside my body, with all my meaningless worries, self-image problems, and everything else I had bottled up inside. I cannot think of a better way to explain that experience than something brutally sobering – as if all of a sudden something opened my eyes to a completely different reality, even though it only lasted for a split second.

As I returned to my body, I made a very uncharacteristic decision: I accepted that it was not going to happen that day and I relieved myself of the self-imposed training duty. Being an amateur sports hobbyist, it was utter nonsense that I let my momentary physical performance control the way I felt, how satisfied I was, and that I allowed it to determine whether I accepted myself or liked myself. I jogged home, took a shower, and went to bed.

The Ironman and the Family-Work Balance

I had already been living off of my investments at the time of my Ironman preparation and, as part of my individual enterprise, was teaching others how to achieve that kind of financial independence through my book and online video courses. Having no set work time or children to look after, I was easily able to train during the day. Nevertheless, there were plenty of people in our triathlon club who did have to balance their training with their family and work obligations. It was a question of determination and organization, and since many people are able to do it, it is clearly not impossible. Since I had a choice, I always tried to get my daily training done as early as possible, usually in the morning hours, so that I didn't have any of those distressing "you have training to do" thoughts lingering around all day.

This is Not Going to Work! I Need Help!

Although this was a defining experience, I must disclose that it did not "cure" me. The following day I went back and completed the 10x1000, but I also recognized that this marathon was not going to be one for the books. I had decided not to continue with the torturous interval runs and instead would do my usual long runs by the creek. I had my experience on Monday. I still did the interval session on Tuesday, and on Wednesday I did a light 22-miler in the name of "change." It was far from sane, similar to the other training sessions I had logged in my Garmin's memory bank back then; it was no surprise that I completely sabotaged my marathon performance.

Nevertheless, I had been shaken deeply enough by an outside force to see that if I really wanted sports to become part of my life, without permanently damaging myself in the process, and I was crazy enough to set the Ironman in my sights, then I needed to ask for expert help. Never mind that I had had that at my disposal all along and never taken advantage of it. Better later than never, I guess.

The Fast Lane

As the goal realization recipe has already shown via the drawing course, wherever it is possible, it is always a good idea to seek help from those who have already been to where you would like to go. On one hand, many detours can be avoided by acquiring the knowledge and support of such people, hence significantly shortening the project, and on the other hand, the chances of success greatly increase.

Luckily, it is relatively easy to acquire expert guidance in amateur sports. The results can easily be measured, felt, and assessed to reassure you that you are on the right track. What more could you wish for, right?

Confessions of an Ironman

> I greatly profited from using professional help in sports. In the realm of investments, I had to find my own path, learning from internationally renowned investors and following their guidance. I could easily write a book about the painfully expensive and harshly extreme adventures I endured while learning the profession in Hungary, but since only about half of the frauds and hoaxers have been placed behind bars, I am going to keep those illuminating stories to myself for the time being.

I don't think they knew much about me at the triathlon club, as I only went there to swim three times a week. They might have assumed, given my Budapest 70.3 result, that I had a bike and a pair of running shoes.

It was around mid-September, after a morning swim practice, when I stepped up to Ákos, the coach, and I told him that I wanted to do an Ironman the following year and needed a training plan. I had made a serious commitment and there was not a single question in my mind that I would reach my goal in 2016. (Do you remember? Integrity! I mind my words and when I say something, I follow through.) We didn't discuss much then, I merely told him that I knew nothing about training methodology, had no idea how recovery worked or how long it took, similar to my ignorance in sports nutrition or even the proper workout frequency which could ensure that I advanced my fitness while not killing myself in the process. I could not really gauge how much knowledge Ákos had as a coach at the time, but I felt that I was going to be in good hands and that my preparation was going to be very different. What that meant was still a mystery to me, but I was certain that my mindless self-torture had come to an end.

The first shocking surprise came on the 23rd of September when I sat down for my "project kickoff" meeting with Ákos. That thirty-

This is Not Going to Work! I Need Help!

minute talk shed light on many of my earlier mistakes. Ákos told me that my training plan would involve cycles, meaning that a three-week higher intensity period would be followed by a recovery week, the purpose of which was to give my body time to process the work done. In addition to that, I would also have a rest day each week and another day with a lighter workload. (This ended up being Friday, when I was free after the morning swim.) Ákos further deepened my shock by saying that it wasn't necessary to go all-out each time I had a training session because the measure of the quality of the session was not based on how wiped out I became. I had no idea what I was getting into, but it certainly seemed much better than my own senseless and cruel training program.

We discussed what kind of a weekly workload I was already used to and how much time I could devote to training altogether. Being self-employed, my schedule was flexible. I had no restrictions whatsoever and based on my Garmin stats, it looked as though I could feasibly handle 10-hour training weeks from the beginning. Ákos' guidelines pointed toward an 8-hour-ish training week to start with, which he thought we could increase to about 15 hours as we progressed. (We ended up exceeding that by quite a bit.) I needed a performance diagnostic test, too, and the data could help formulate a heart rate- and pace-based training program.

Petrified by the overwhelming amount of new information, I posed a reckless question, "What do you think would be a realistic finishing time for me for an Ironman?" The way I understood it, one had to complete the 2.4-mile swim, 112-mile bike and the 26.2-mile run in 16 hours in order to be officially declared an Ironman. (Since then, I learned that different courses may have different time limits.) Obviously, I wanted a faster finishing time, but to be completely honest, I didn't dare to imagine anything better than around a 13-hour result.

One by one, we looked at every race result I had had and then Ákos came up with a number that I had trouble identifying with for quite

Confessions of an Ironman

some time. "If all falls into place, I can imagine a time right around the 11:30 mark." "How did you come to this number?" came my immediate response, even though I was not sure that I was ready to hear the background figures. One of the anchors for the math was that my biking still had a lot of room for improvement, and the other was that my marathon results looked good already, which meant that the calculation involved an assumption of a sub 4-hour marathon. Additionally, as a result of the three practices per week, I would certainly make improvements on the swim front, too, so 11:30 wasn't farfetched – according to Ákos.

His answer haunted me from that moment on. The 11:30 finishing time became permanently nested in my head. It could be that Ákos deliberately did that, as a result of keen psychological considerations, but it could have also been that he just did some straightforward math and those were simply the figures he came up with. We closed our conversation by agreeing that I would start the systematic preparations in the second half of November, as I had already scheduled a three-week "vacation" with Anikó after the Budapest Marathon.

Mental Anchoring

This expression refers to a cognitive bias in decision-making in which we put too much emphasis on factoring in information we initially received about a given topic. A simple example of that is the classic price negotiation. An introductory price provided by a good salesman may be far off the real value of a given good, yet most people still use that number as the base when they begin to bargain. The salesman has already won, before the bargaining begins. What comes after in the actual back-and-forth is nothing more than an act, which, for instance, is played with intense artistry at the Grand Bazaar in Istanbul all day long.

This is Not Going to Work! I Need Help!

The anchor's distorting effect is unbelievably potent in decision-making. Amos Tversky and Daniel Kahneman – pioneers in behavioral economics – conducted an experiment in 1974 in which they first spun a fortune wheel that had numbers 1 through 100 on it. They deliberately set the wheel to only stop on either 10 or 65. Once the wheel stopped on a number, they asked the subjects to estimate whether the percentage of African nations in the UN is greater or smaller than the figure on the wheel (10% or 65%). For the next step, everyone had to give a specific percentage as well. And here comes the main point: Those whose numbers turned out to be 10% after the spin, guesstimated 25% on average, but those who ended up with the 65% anchor figure voted for 45% on average. As far as they knew, the number that the wheel stopped on was completely random, and had absolutely no rational connection with the inquiry that followed. Yet, the answers showed that individuals could not let the number go when asked to make an "independent decision."

Looking at my case, the 11:30 time goal did not appear to have a whole lot to do with reality, either. But the anchor was set, no doubt about that, even if it was not a conscious decision by Ákos.

For the remainder of time until the race, I did my preparations alone, paying a few visits to my track for some self-inflicted torture, but mostly doing moderately-paced long runs by the creek. The October 11, 2015, Budapest Marathon is not deserving of a dedicated chapter – it was merely the last nail in the coffin of my old training ways. Had there still been a single question, whether or not I should carry on with my preparations more sensibly, using expert advice, minding what my body told me while following those basic rules I knew nothing about, this running race would have convinced me of that beyond any doubt.

Confessions of an Ironman

If I had to go by my emotions, that was the most miserable marathon I have ever run. It might give an idea how badly I paced myself when I tell you that I coupled a 1-hour 40-minute half marathon with almost two hours of torture to complete the second half, going through unthinkable suffering in the last 11 miles or so. I wanted to improve on my time from Rome; all I would have needed was to keep about a 9:10 per mile pace over the last 3 miles, but I could not even do that. The reason why I wrote earlier that I "sabotaged" this marathon was because, all the way through, I kept telling myself, "I have not prepared properly for this, therefore I don't deserve a better result." In the end, after all the pain, I managed a 3-hour 36-minute finish time, just like in Rome. To be exact, I beat my time by 9 seconds, but being in the state I was in, I was incapable of celebrating. As far as I was concerned, I got what I deserved.

We didn't stick around for long after my finish. I was feeling very much the tortured victim who wasn't far from shedding a tear in the car on the way home due to the pain inflicted by my bottomless self-pity. There was nothing to whine about; I was simply stupid! I could have done a better job preparing and could have raced smarter, too. Not to mention that no one had stood in my way to prevent me from finding expert help much sooner.

I didn't train in anything but swimming for two weeks after the race. We then went to Sri Lanka for three weeks. I was so exhausted that I could have easily slept through the entire vacation if there hadn't been so many things to see. I was also restless because I knew there was no turning back: I had made my commitment to completing the Ironman, although I still saw it as a nearly impossible feat. I did not know what difference a professional training plan was going to make in my life, and I had no clue what to expect during the months ahead. It made me very nervous.

This is Not Going to Work! I Need Help!

Could You Be Happy for a 3% Chance?

Allan Pease, who is perhaps best known for *The Definitive Book of Body Language*, had been diagnosed with cancer. His doctor had indicated that patients with his diagnosis statistically had a 3% chance of survival. It was astonishing to listen to him during a presentation as he led us through his thought process, explaining why he was actually happy with that number! He was convinced beyond a doubt that the 3% who survived were not the result of some sort of accident; they had to have done something differently from the rest. He told his doctor that the way he saw it, all he had to do was to map out the survival strategies of those among the 3% and copy their recipe. He knew it was his choice which group he was to join and he chose the surviving group; he began his research and radically changed his lifestyle.[9] The decision to which group you wish to belong is entirely up to you in all aspects of your life! All you need to do is map out the habits of those who are part of that group and do what they do. You're not the only one who wants to become rich, who wants to become an Ironman, who wants to fight off an illness... There is no need to reinvent the wheel, just be open to change and take the driver's seat.

There is a thought that came from Christian Darnel, a philosopher, author, and trainer, which I very much embrace. He said that the reason why so many people are stuck on one orbit is because they are unable to accept that their future is totally empty. Anything could happen the next day, truly anything! Hence, the best thing would be to picture the future as a blank page and fill it with drawings of one's desires, manifesting

---

[9] I sent Allan Pease an e-mail, through his publisher, months after his presentation. I knew someone who was faced with a situation where she was in great need of the survival recipe he researched. His reply arrived almost without delay and he sent it to me – to an unknown Hungarian guy – in the form of an excerpt of a book manuscript he was working on at the time. Not too many would have done the same.

Confessions of an Ironman

them. Despite that, most people let their past take over, which, beyond any doubt, is already full and as such, it cannot be altered anymore. Most people take elements of their past that they deem essential for their survival and fill their theoretically empty future with them. If you think that way, you cannot create as you lock yourself in a cage. Before you know it, your nice big sheet of drawing paper is full of elements of your life that you are not quite happy with at the moment. On the other hand, the picture would be much different if you did not assume that the situation you are in is a consequence of something that is out of your control and something that cannot change – like your job, where you live, your health, etc. In order to achieve great goals, to manifest your dream future, it is imperative to be able to think with a blank paper in mind. For admittedly selfish reasons, I regret that Christian is no longer with us. I learned so much from him, and I still have many questions to ask.

Turning back to the drawing course analogy: I asked for a terrifying, A3-sized sheet of paper for July 30th, 2016, the date of the Hungarian national long-distance triathlon championship in Nagyatád. I had no idea how I would create my "exam piece" on it. One ingredient of the success recipe, the expert help, had already been acquired. With the assistance of Ákos I could certainly gain the necessary knowledge; he could also help me break the task into smaller, manageable segments. This goal realization recipe, as described earlier, had previously worked for me. Nevertheless, I felt I was in for a rough ride with a goal of such outrageous magnitude. The probability of success was on my side, however, given that I got it together for the execution.

Is it the Ironman Brand or the Completion That Matters?

There were only fifteen people at the starting line of the very first Ironman. The inaugural race, held in Hawaii on February 18, 1978, was dreamt up by Navy Commander John Collins. The event consisted of a 2.4 mile swim, a 112 mile bike ride, and a 26.2 mile run; only twelve individuals finished the race. The idea was that if anyone could finish such a grueling endeavor, that person was surely worthy of the title "Ironman." Since then, the term Ironman has been turned into a trademarked brand, but it is not only the owner of the brand that organizes triathlon races of the same distance – there are many other triathlons around the world which cover the Ironman distance (140.6 miles).

I am a pathological case when it comes to finisher medals and it had crossed my mind that I should choose a race organized by the authentic Ironman brand, since I was only going to do this once. I was able to convince myself, however, that if someone was capable of completing the distance, regardless of the branding of the race, and as long as it was official, that person was deserving of the Ironman title. There weren't any full- distance races in Hungary under the official Ironman brand, only a 70.3 half-distance event. So, after a little contemplation, that is how I finally chose the Hungarian national championship, which is as official as it gets. They also issued each competitor a certificate of the completion of the Ironman distance. That race had it all, I thought. (Later, just to be on the safe side, I did complete a real Ironman-branded, full-distance race. That, however, is a different story...)

KEEP MOVING ATTITUDE

Granted, I produced some quite laughable scenes, but I think my "self-constructed preparation phase" was an integral part of the journey to reach my goal. This phase could have surely been shortened, but by no means could it have been omitted. In the beginning, asking for outside help was beyond me. It took a while to reach that milestone.

I heard a list at the UPW event in London which perfectly encapsulates the role of my series of stumbles. Here it is:

1. Success is a result of good decisions.

2. Good decisions are a result of experience.

3. Experience comes from a series of bad decisions.

Being brand new to the idea of triathlons, I was totally clueless as to how one needed to prepare for the completion of an Ironman. I could have chosen to just spin my wheels, make no progress, and wait for the perfect solution to fall into my lap. Instead, I chose to remain in constant motion, even when I did not know what I should be doing, because I felt I always needed to make decisions that were in tune with my knowledge at the time, find out what results they might bring, learn from them, and if needed, make the necessary adjustments on my path.

Most people are so afraid of failure that they'd rather avoid diving into anything new, even though failure is an integral part of success.

An abundance of bad decisions – not to mention all the stories which are actually quite funny in hindsight – led me to the point where I decided to ask for expert help.

I think the "stumbling phase" is a very useful one. I am convinced that parents – instead of this paralyzing strive for perfection – should consciously motivate their children to try, and not be afraid to fail! Tony Robbins suggests that parents should provide the starting capital if their children have a "business idea;' for further incentive, they should also add in triple the profit each year. In a model like this, it would be very easy to build the right attitude: The child learns that it is worth it to keep trying until success comes in the end. (The good news for parents is that a child's business ideas are more likely to be along the lines of a lemonade stand in the front yard instead of real estate development.)

My stumbling phase and the overwhelming feelings I had after the Budapest half-distance race, when it became clear that I would not be able to reach my goal by myself, resulted in serious changes. My changes can be viewed through the lens of the following thought-provoking classification: People who have decided to accomplish a big goal can be divided into three different groups, based on what they do once they hit a plateau, after passing the initial, steep phase of the learning curve.

1. A large number cannot handle stagnation, so their remedy will be quitting; they'll move on to a different goal. Those who think that way rarely overcome mediocrity and will never be able to create anything great because this stalling, stagnating phase is part of all journeys that lead to great goals. Hence, it can never be avoided.

2. Those not willing to settle for mediocrity, and who persevere by staying on the path toward their goal, may decide to push even harder, handling the stagnation phase with increased energy input until they push through and break out of that grueling phase. Those coming from this group are not the type who give

Confessions of an Ironman

up, but they cannot really enjoy their success because they completely drain themselves along the way. Based on what I've written in the first half of this book, I was a classic example of this group when in my self-constructed, independent preparation phase.

3. Members of the third group are the truly conscious warriors. They anticipate the arrival of the stagnation phase. Instead of letting it unnerve them, they find ways to overcome it, including seeking outside help. A willingness to learn from others who understand the adversities we might encounter may not only shorten the time to reach our goals, but can also help keep our energy exertion in check so that we can ultimately enjoy our success.

One of the positive yields of the Ironman was that I fled the always-grumbling, nothing-is-ever-good-enough, self-torturing second group and joined the third one. To do that, though, I had to fall into all the traps of the second group, exhaust all its resources, and receive the uncomfortable shocks, first. I would not have been able to make that shift any sooner.

MISTAKES THROUGH THE EYES OF AN EXPERT: I WENT DOWN THE LIST AND DIDN'T MISS ONE

Ákos made it clear that I had experienced most of the mistakes that an amateur athlete training alone can make. Not only that, but I also managed to intensify many of them to extreme levels.

Obsessive compulsive training. The expression "light training" was not in my vocabulary, nor was "planned recovery time." My preparation only included the "as much as I can, as hard as I can" approach. Work done in the easy zone, which should be executed with lower heart rates and low intensity, the purpose of which is to train the heart and the circulatory system, was completely missing from my repertoire. From my incompetent point of view, it seemed completely useless to take it easy when running. That kind of training, which trains our so-called lipid metabolism, is the backbone of the preparation for long-distance endurance events such as the Ironman, improving our stamina in the process. Simply put, the result of this training is an increased pace that we can maintain for long periods of time. (A fit athlete's lactic acid levels will

Confessions of an Ironman

only start to rise at a higher intensity, which means that this person can sustain higher intensity work for longer. I knew nothing about this when I was training on my own.)

Graduality, regularity, and consistency. It is not difficult to assume that if the body is exposed to something that it is not used to, it will get a shock. It is obvious that it was an insane idea to launch my running career with a half-marathon on Margaret Island because a sudden workload of that scale could easily result in injury. I was lucky to have gotten away without any serious problems (considering all my crazy ideas). Going by the theory of graduality, the wise thing would have been to increase both the intensity and the duration of training little by little, taking small incremental steps toward the goal. My self-created marathon plan, which ended up being a failure, was as far from this approach as possible. Neither did I know that the stimuli I exposed my body to were way too rare and inconsistent, which made it impossible for me to improve. Experts say that allowing 3-5 days to pass between training sessions renders basically everything one does completely useless. To sum it up, the regularity and the consistency of the training sessions, along with the careful consideration of the cycles of hard work and recovery, are imperative to being able to make progress. The latter, I think, is impossible to plan right without a skilled professional. (If you are interested in the subject, do a search on the term *supercompensation*. I must admit, I turned numb for a while when I began to understand what those interconnected waves meant and when I discovered their astounding contrast with what I called training when I was preparing for races on my own.)

Recovery. Ákos indicated that it could take weeks for an athlete to recover enough to perform at the same level as before a half Ironman or marathon. After hearing that, I didn't have too many questions left regarding whether it had been a "smart" idea to go out to my track and do those "thousands" a mere two days after the very first half Ironman of my life, or to run a marathon within a week. I had no clue that there was a training category called recovery session (basically going easy at about 50% of the maximum intensity), which, when paired with the adequate amount of rest and sleep, is instrumental in speeding up the recovery period. None of these three elements had been included in my training equation.

Rhythm and cyclicality. Ideally, a training plan that involves gradually increasing workloads, and which is geared toward the attainment of a long-term goal, has a rhythm and cyclicality to which the "undergoing" athlete's body progressively gets used to. Regarding rhythm, in one training week three days of intensive work are usually followed by an easier day, and then two harder days with an easy day as closure. Seldom are there more than three days of high intensity work in a row within each discipline, even among top athletes. How fortunate that triathlon consists of three sports, because all I should have kept in mind was not to drain myself with the same sport on consecutive days! My home track acts or those circuit rides are classic illustrations of my failure on these fronts (as well). In alignment with cyclicality, a two- or three-week higher intensity training period should be followed by a lighter week, so that the workload can be processed by the body. As a result, when the hard work restarts after the recovery period, the athlete can start from a higher fitness level than before. This, like almost everything else, was new information for me.

I could go on in length, sounding smart, about how the trinity of the cardiovascular system, mitochondria, and the capillary system is the foundation of superior athletic performance, and how these components can be trained specifically. The very essence of training in various heart rate zones is that there are different physiological processes that take place in those different zones, therefore the physiological effects of these trainings are also going to differ. As time passed, I began to understand this, but due to a lack of deeper interest, I never dove into the subject, instead I purchased personalized, instant help.

Confessions of an Ironman

Even Though I Don't Get it, I Can Still Use it!

"Pick the fruit first, study the roots later." This saying perfectly sums up that one does not need to study electricity wholeheartedly and understand it in order to use it. It is just enough to find the switch to begin with.

I was the same way with the training plan. Initially, I had no idea what the underlying principles were. I just began to follow the plan, knowing that I could always look into the scientific background if I happened to be so inclined.

One thing I must add to this equation of success is the determination, the decision. And I certainly don't mean a "let's give it a try" attitude by this, but the kind of irrevocable commitment which makes any sort of plan B superfluous; the one that burns bridges and only allows for forward movement. This is the only kind of determination that I call a decision and, based on my experience, a series of these sort of *real* decisions make our lives what they are. The starting of my own business, the departure from the operational management of it, and the focus on investing and teaching, these decisions all definitely fall into this category, just like my commitment to the Ironman.

III. ON A CONTROLLED PATH

A NEW ERA AND MANY SURPRISES

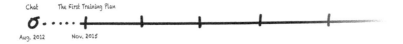

I received my first training plan on November 15, 2015, after we returned home from Sri Lanka. It was packed with directives which, to say the least, were out of my comfort zone.

Right off the bat, I attended a Monday gym session with other athletes, complete with running drills, Total Body Resistance (TRX) exercises, and heaps of various core-strengthening exercises. As I had never done any form of training that involved targeting those specific muscle groups, the first time was a shock to my system. I can honestly say, without exaggeration, all I could do was try to survive. I could handle the introductory running drills, but even those totally wiped me out. My first encounter with the TRX bands turned out to be pretty interesting. Having to keep the bands tight the whole time, while trying not to engage my hips, was a bit much for me all at once. The plank stands made me feel as though I was working myself towards a slow and exhausting death.

When you try an entirely new type of motion, it is natural that it will be strenuous in the beginning as it takes time to adapt. The strength training was very hard for the first few occasions; as time passed, I grew to handle it better and better. It became less and less necessary to reserve my energy so that I could leave the gym on my

A New Era and Many Surprises

own two feet instead of having to be carried out. After a few weeks, I was looking forward to starting my training weeks with these evening group sessions. These practices remained on my weekly schedule all the way up to the race with rare exceptions.

It is not necessary to list all the details of my 37-week training plan; it would be just as boring to summarize as it would be to read. During the first week, however, I stalled at almost every element of my new plan. Those details are much more interesting.

After the Monday training party it felt good to have a Tuesday morning swim, after which I was to go out for a 40 minute easy run on flat roads. My only problem was that I did not know what an easy tempo meant; every time I had gone out to run on my own, I ran really hard. Furthermore, the way I saw it then, it was useless to put on running shoes for a mere 40 minute jog. I was totally dumbfounded by the whole concept, but I still did it. Later, I learned the "scientific" background behind the process.

On Wednesday I had to get out my bike and, literally, dust it off. I hadn't ridden since the half- distance triathlon of August. The assignment was an hour of light spinning at a cadence over 90 revolutions per minute. The "light spinning" function was also absent from my toolkit; I was also lacking a cadence meter. I called Ákos and we agreed that I should go ahead and count it myself. I went out to my good old stadium circuit and actually counted how many revolutions my pedals made in a minute in the beginning and then simply tried to keep that pace, inserting a "control count" here and there. There were many feelings that ensued: First of all, it had been a bad idea to abandon my bike for so long because we had become complete strangers. Second, returning from Sri Lanka in the middle of November, the weather felt exceptionally cold. By the second half of the ride, the wind had gotten so strong that it almost blew me off the tarmac. Third, it was obvious that "counting in the head" was a one-time solution. I had to hit the town and find some sort of Garmin accessory.

Confessions of an Ironman

The next session was the usual morning swim on Thursday, with an interval running session with the team that same evening. This Thursday program was more or less fixed on my calendar, the "only" thing that varied was the content. On Fridays I only had swimming – that was my lighter day because after the early morning program I was able to rest. We did a time trial in the first week and I swam a 7-minute 30-second 400 meter (about 437 yards). (If you have ever done anything like that, this may show you at what level I was.)

I had to collect myself for the weekend because the Saturday program was running in the hills, along with the core exercises to be done at home, and on Sunday I was to ride for two hours on hilly terrain. I had not seen any hills or mountains around my house. I am from the countryside originally and was not familiar with the area at all. Consequently, my first thought was that I would go and run at the only hill I knew in the city, Gellért Hill. "Hill" is in its name, I thought, and I had already gone there a few times in my college years and it seemed pretty steep, as far as I could recall. On the first Saturday I was only supposed to run 50 minutes, but the truth is that it didn't take me but a few steps to find out why the street I parked on was literally called "Sweat Street." When I glanced at my watch, already gasping for air, to see how much more I had to endure, it showed that precisely 1 minute 34 seconds had passed; I had quite a bit of time remaining before I hit the 50 minute mark. Somehow, I managed to complete the run. Sunday evening, when I was sending my training plan back along with my feedback, I put the following thoughts down describing my very first hill run: "I ended up on Gellért Hill, and since I had never done anything like that before, it wiped me out. Is there a special technique I should know when running uphill?" On the one hand, it does have a technique, which we discussed later; on the other hand, I was told that I had guts going to Gellért Hill. But since I still remained without knowledge of the surrounding area, I stuck with it all the way through, because at least I didn't get lost on the way there. After the first occasion, I had

A New Era and Many Surprises

a good running route which apparently was perfect for the training session prescribed.

I was just as afraid of Sunday as I was of Saturday, because I was certain that I could not ride for two hours in the cold November weather. After going through some trouble and a lot of bargaining, I put my hands on a Tacx Ironman virtual reality trainer, which was more expensive than my bike. I had to follow the training program because I had already made my commitment to it. This was my best hope because it was the type of trainer that could emulate any course, automatically adjusting the resistance on the rear wheel, slowing it down when the road was ascending, making it harder to pedal, and speeding up when on a downhill section. Additionally, it was quite enjoyable that I was able to ride the Hawaii Ironman course, which came included in the package, right in my living room. I could put the recorded picture of the bike course on my TV on the wall and the picture was even moving in tune with my actual speed. The gear was professional; I wasn't quite yet, but I could improve upon that. The first week was all about countless stimuli that put me outside of my comfort zone. I had to try new things (strength training, hill runs, easy runs, light spinning on the bike, using a home trainer) and also had to acquire all the necessary equipment.

Our coordinated effort in executing the training plan was such that on each Sunday, after the completion of my last session, I sent my feedback to Ákos along with a written comment in the beginning, and I also attached the Garmin link of each activity, so that he could see all the details, too. I usually received the following week's program that evening as well. (In case you're looking for the heralded rest day in my program, just as I was trying to find it at first, then let me tell you that if the Sunday rides were scheduled for the morning, between that time and the Monday strength trainings, and I quote, "There are more than 24 hours for recovery, even if there aren't any specific, calendar rest days per se.")

Confessions of an Ironman

At Least the Home Trainer is an Ironman!

I had looked at the Tacx Ironman brand virtual reality trainer before the trip to Sri Lanka, but a few things kept me from buying it at the time. For one, it was way too expensive and, perhaps because of that, it was a rare commodity. Plus, I wasn't simply looking for a place I could walk in, put it in a shopping cart, and walk out again. I wanted to try it out first. If I liked it, I also wanted it for the best possible price. Those qualifications made the task difficult.

As a first step, I contacted the Hungarian distributor, who was very helpful and provided me with a test machine by sending it to a bike shop of my choosing in Budapest. By Murphy's Law, it arrived when I was on my vacation abroad, although I did tell them when and how long I'd be gone. By the time I got back, the indoor trainer had found its way back to the distributor. There was nothing I could do but start from scratch again, even though I was really pressed for time because of the training plan.

Finally, I managed to try out the machine in the bike shop, where the crew willingly confessed that it took them multiple attempts before they could set it up. I was not getting a very reassuring feeling. It turned out that one of the guys at the shop used to be on our national cycling team and he thought that any person willing to spend that much on a professional indoor trainer must be at least around his level. As a result, he didn't think twice about selecting a course that was filled with beautiful, mountainous sections, winding through some forested land. He had a good time watching me ride, no question about that. I, on the other hand, didn't need more than a couple of minutes to be near death. It was a good thing that I had a change of clothes with me.

The machine, beyond any doubt, could deliver what I needed: Its transitions between inclines and downhills were very smooth,

A New Era and Many Surprises

and, had I been a proper cyclist and didn't have to keep all my focus on staying alive, it could have even provided me with some aesthetic pleasure with its breathtaking pictures on the monitor. The only thing I didn't like was how much that trainer cost. After some talking, the manager was ready to reduce the price by almost 25% – which meant a savings of well over 300 dollars. (Just like I make sure I only buy attractively priced shares of high-quality companies when investing, I also apply the same principles in all my other purchases, which I am sure brightens up everyone's day who are ever lucky enough to be involved in the given transaction.) From that point, my only problem was that there was another store where the package I was looking at was still at a lower price, which also included a "complementary" DVD of the Hawaii Ironman bike course.

I felt that the fair thing was to come straight out and show the shop that allowed me to test the machine what the competitor's offer was, and if they were willing to match that, I would make the purchase there. In the end, I managed to acquire that wonder in the nick of time, and at a much better price than what was publicly advertised anywhere. "We" were ready to share some adventures...

A PARALLEL PROJECT

I always followed the training plan I was given as accurately as possible. For one, I consider it a question of attitude (that is how I am); also, the reason I asked for a professional's guidance was because he knew how to help me reach my goal, and I didn't have the necessary knowledge to second-guess in any way what he prescribed. Additionally, why ask for a training plan if I wasn't going to follow it?! Having to stay in touch and regularly send training data back might be motivating for some, but I was not very interested in that aspect of our collaboration. For me, it was merely a part of the assignment: I only considered a task done when – given that it made sense – I wrote down a few thoughts about it, and copied the related Garmin link into the Sunday feedback document.

Although this rigid, systematic approach was no doubt beneficial for my preparation, I still felt quite restricted in other areas of my life where I applied the same inflexible, painstakingly systematic approach. By that time, I had been seeing a therapist-like helper for a while. I have to say that I strongly agree with the statement that everyone ought to have conversations with a psychologist on a regular basis. Although she was not a psychologist, many deeply buried thoughts emerged, thanks to her. During the first week of my work with the new training plan, for instance, she seemed convinced that my reason for doing this Ironman was to punish myself for not being *good enough*. She bluntly said that I ought to ask for a whip, too, to go right along with the training plan, because that would really make my self-torture complete.

Nonetheless, no matter what I managed to dig up from the depths of my mind during our sessions, there was no question that I would finish what I had started, meaning that there was no one and nothing that could deter me from the Ironman. As previously noted, I might be influenced or even convinced to change my mind during the phase that preceded a decision, but once the decision had been made, there was no stopping me until I achieved what I had set my mind to.

Had it not been for this work on myself, which went parallel with the training, my Ironman project might have simply ended up as a means to collect one more finisher medal (making writing about it quite superfluous, too). This way, however, it became my vehicle which, by the time I reached the finish line, took me to a place where I was able to put down my compulsive performance anxiety. Make no mistake, working on oneself, digging up one's deeply rooted, underlying motivations is immeasurably harder than running up any hills or riding the Hawaii Ironman bike course. I had to face such questions as, "Why is it good for me that my training plan completely fills my week and gets me sufficiently exhausted?" "What am I running from?" "Does it have anything to do with my relationships?" "Do I only feel worthy as long as I am actively involved in something?"

Unfortunately, I never met a sports psychologist during my preparation, so I can only go by my instincts when I voice my opinion that most people who are constantly chasing medals, records, and ceaselessly raising the bar by looking for more and more difficult challenges, should gather the courage to face the real challenge: Themselves. An active lifestyle is great, but I am convinced that looking within is the only way life can become really fulfilling.

WITHOUT EATING OR SLEEPING

The questions which emerged during the first phase of my new training plan as a result of my perhaps overly intensified journey of self-discovery made me feel so awful that I had trouble sleeping and eating. That made it even more difficult to complete my sessions as prescribed, but I didn't look for excuses. I kept following the training plan.

From the second week on, I used the virtual trainer to do my "easy spinning" sessions, too. I could set a completely flat city course and see all my data on the screen, including my heart rate, cadence, and speed. This enabled me to train in a much more comfortable environment, and be able to execute my assignments with much more precision, as opposed to going outside to suffer in the cold. My weekend rides were always done Hawaiian style and it was as if I had to fight for my life right in the middle of my living room. The Ironman bike course did not lack difficult hills or downhill sections and it served my development well.

I found the interval running sessions with the team positively enjoyable, not only because I happened to be one of the faster runners, but also because my teammates gave me a lot of useful information and helpful advice. I learned, for instance, during a warm-up that the time Ákos forecasted for me was unusually fast for a person about to attempt the race for the first time. Not only that, but it was also said that many people in the field, with the exception of the professionals, would be very happy with an 11:30 finishing time. Although I had had a similar hunch, I was still so far removed from the notion of completing the race that I didn't think too much about how fast I would finish. (It was much later that I started to actively think about the time, only after I felt that my goal seemed to be within reach.)

A Parallel Project

Do You Ever Stop to Celebrate?

Generally, when I come close to reaching a goal, I immediately start my search for the next, bigger, and more distant ambition, instead of taking the time to properly celebrate my accomplishment. It is undeniable that positive feedback is extremely important, and one can very easily become enmeshed in a depleting series of endless goals without it. For example, as I was getting close to the completion of my Ironman project, I started formulating a multi-level goal structure, which went way beyond the "simple" idea of completing the distance.

It is sort of like when a little kid is convinced that the good life will start once he or she grows up. Reaching school age, kids realize that they still aren't very hip after all – but continue to think that if they wait until they are older and on their own, they'll be free to do whatever they want. Once adulthood arrives, and work takes over and consumes their lives, they begin to look forward to retirement; being an adult is not quite as liberating as initially believed. Once retirement hits, awakening finally knocks on the door: Life was great, as a child or a young adult, but instead of the perpetual longing for something different that the future would bring, it would have been nice to recognize the good things and the beauty of the present moment. I once saw a sign while walking on Venice Beach in Los Angeles, California: "Don't grow up, it's a trap." The importance of living in the moment, and celebrating success and achievement, cannot be overstated.

The slogan of the Nagyatád long-distance triathlon, "The Journey is the Goal Itself," is true indeed. You should always strive to find the beauty in what you are doing at any given moment of the preparation (or life, for that matter). At one time, for instance, as I was finishing up one of my lonely rides, I spotted an elderly lady riding her worn down bicycle, laden with a sizable basket. The sun was beating down pretty hard, and

Confessions of an Ironman

although by that time I was quite tired, my spark of motivation was clear: "I'll pass her before the next hill." I realized that while I was going over 19 mph, the old lady was slowly pulling away from me riding her small-wheeled, weighed-down bike. I quickly popped a power gel and went on with my mental wrestling game, thinking perhaps I'd be better off if I "signed her for my sports team" and partnered with this more-than-likely pensioner to complete the Ironman in a relay, where she'd be handling the bike leg for me. It was humiliating that I couldn't even get close to her, let alone pass her. We were way past the hill I originally picked as the spot where she'd be behind me, and my power gel supplies were almost as low as my spirits, when I realized that this elderly "female athlete" was making me sweat like there was no tomorrow without even moving her legs. Finally, as she pulled over near a bridge – she had arrived home with her pack, I presumed – I got a chance to take a closer look. I realized that my undertaking was no less than passing a motorized bicycle.

Our experiences, both good and bad, lend real beauty to reaching our goals but it is important to allow ourselves to stop and recognize each little triumph along the way. The importance of the latter is something I constantly remind myself.

Another time, during warm-up laps before a running practice, I was picking the brain of a multiple Ironman finisher, investigating what his most valuable learnings were that helped him improve his performance. He told me that it took him numerous completions before he found out the real secret. Naturally, I did not let up and went on with my inquiry to find out that, in his opinion, the secret lay in the nutrition plan on the bike ride. His success recipe meant dissolving as many packs of energy gel as possible in a bottle of water – he said 6-8, as I recall – and that's how it should be consumed with calculated timing, while also making sure to take an adequate amount of clear water on board with it. This information

A Parallel Project

was brand new to me. I had certainly heard before that coming up with the right nutrition plan was regarded as the fourth discipline of a long-distance triathlon, and I also knew it was no joke, which I got to experience firsthand when completing the half-distance race. My problem was that I have a very sensitive stomach and having never used power gels before, I had serious doubts that I could actually keep anything like that down. Nonetheless, enlightened by his wisdom, the knowledge was now mine that I needed about 6-8 packs of that stuff in me if I wanted to get off the bike with realistic hope that I could tackle the marathon. I was in for some adventures testing that out, but at least someone got me inside the circle of "wisdom." (Later, of course, I learned everyone has their own secret they swear by and nutrition is one topic where it is very difficult to find two people with identical takes on the subject. Since I was the one with the least amount of experience, no matter what I heard, I paid attention to it.)

You Will Become Like Those You Spend Your Time With

I have always been more of the solitary type who tends to turn inward, constantly thinking. During my Ironman preparation, however, I got a taste of working with my peers and came to recognize the undeniable benefits. It is always good to have someone to learn from, to hear what those with more experience have to say. Previously, what held me back from joining any group training sessions was that I presumed to be way behind everyone, even though I had no idea where they were. As a result, I didn't really want to work with them. Since my karate club days, belonging to a club felt foreign to me. During my Ironman adventure, however, I could see that being part of a team contributed a lot to my learning process.

Tony Robbins said that people's lives are a direct reflection of the expectations of their peer group. With that said, we

> must be wise when we decide with whom we wish to surround ourselves. Contrary to popular belief, Tony does not believe in the supportive environment. Rather, his encouragement is to surround ourselves with people who present us with challenges, through which we can improve. A good sports club has that function, without exposing the individual to unhealthy and harmful comparisons. If you want to become an Ironman, train with those who already have that title! If you strive for financial freedom, try to stay near people who have already achieved that and learn from them! There is hardly a better recipe, regardless of your goal.

My running was clearly getting better, despite the fact that getting back into the groove after Sri Lanka had been very difficult. I became a regular guest on Gellért Hill, running to the summit, not holding back one bit on those arduous hills, doing 3-4 repeats at a time, as per the duration requirements of my training plan. Additionally, it was also revealed during our interval sessions that there was way more to them than just the "thousands" – the variations in distances, the target pace, and intensity could open the door to infinite diversity, and lead to gradual improvement. The key word here being gradual...far from what I had been doing on my own. I liked these training sessions because they were tuned in a way that always allowed me, even if just barely, to stay afloat and not die and, consequently, to get stronger and faster with each passing week.

My biggest burden at that time was that I could only sleep about 2-3 hours a day. Meanwhile, the training put me under sizable physical strain, which was probably the reason why I was so looking forward to the rest week that was to close the first training cycle. When I saw the program prescribed for that week, however, I was hit with the harsh reality that the word "rest" had a wide spectrum of meanings. The training plan seemed to largely resemble the mileage of the first week, which had not felt easy at all.

IN CASE I GOT USED TO IT ...

The training plan was perfect, because as soon as I felt I was getting comfortable with my regular assignments and the mileages, a change was introduced, which either upped quotas or added something that pushed me slightly outside my comfort zone again. The increases in the workloads and the introduction of additional, new elements remained gradual, so I can only recall a couple of occasions throughout the entire preparation when I got a little bit of a shock: In the very beginning, when practically everything was new, and in the spring, right at the beginning of the new "act" entitled, "Let's get the bike out and put in some real mileage."

The Lesson of the Chinese Bamboo

Inherently, I like to have an idea of what path a given project is supposed to follow, so I would have appreciated a chance to see my months-long training plan in its entirety as opposed to the "weekly dosage." However, I also felt many times that it was a blessing in disguise to have it revealed to me that way. Working through each session, it was always the very next one that seemed to be on the edge of what I felt was attainable for my level. Had I been confronted with the workloads that were planned for the last phase of my preparations ahead of time, it is quite likely I would have gotten anxious and start-

Confessions of an Ironman

ed second-guessing myself. (I felt the same way about writing my first book or creating my online video courses, too. Had I known what I was getting into, I might not have launched either of those projects.)

To be successful, to create great things, all one needs to do is take a dive without overcomplicating and overthinking, focusing only on the tasks of the given day, striving for the best possible way to complete those and nothing else. The Nike slogan: "Just do it!" works well if executed along the lines of a sensibly designed plan, a carefully constructed recipe. Nevertheless, the daily portion has to be done, even when you don't see all the way to the end of the road, when you don't particularly like the current results and the final destination seems completely out of reach. In my experience, all big projects have those phases when everything seems to be beyond hope, when it is pitch black in the "tunnel" and the end is unfathomable, and it becomes questionable whether it makes sense to continue the pursuit. But at times like these, you still put in the necessary amount of work, then slowly (sometimes very slowly) but surely the picture becomes clear again. For that to happen, though, one must persevere.

However uncharacteristic it seems, I deserted writing this book several times, simply because I did not see any sense in continuing it; I was unsure that it could actually add value to anyone's life. Once I made the irrevocable decision that I would finish it no matter what, I made a commitment to write at least one hour every day. This recipe has always worked for me.

I have come across a fable in books and various seminars in which a certain type of Chinese bamboo is mentioned. The uniqueness of this particular plant lies in the fact that once its seed has been planted, it needs to be nurtured daily for a very long time – for years, possibly – when all the while it gives no sign of life whatsoever, without any trace of a single seedling poking through the ground. The presence of the nurturing care has to remain without any positive reinforcement coming back to the caretaker; water has to be poured over it solely based on inner beliefs, otherwise it will die. The reward of commitment and perseverance comes much later, but when that moment finally arrives, the plant takes off growing at an unprecedented rate and easily makes up for the lag, compensating for all that it has been given. This plant – which might very well be the product of imagination for the sake of the story – would most probably die in the majority of cases as there are so few who have the attitude needed to keep it alive.

The truth is, all great projects work exactly the same way: Whether it is writing a book, preparing for the Ironman, or targeting financial freedom, they all require the continuous, daily work to reach the big goal. When on the road to becoming an investor, my work was one hour of reading every day – that is how I put together the functioning recipe. They say that long-term investing is essentially an endurance sport, and since I feel at home with both of them, I can confidently say that this parallel is as accurate as can be. The road to success is the same in both cases.

The shocking experience of the second training block was the performance diagnostics test where various measurements of a number of life functions are taken (breathing and heart rate) and a few drops of blood are drawn from the earlobe with certain regularity, while the subject is on an indoor trainer, pedaling on a course that is continuously getting more and more difficult. After the biking part, the subject has to immediately switch to a treadmill and the show goes on. These facts were all I knew before I underwent the procedure. As if it wasn't hard enough, it was exponentially more difficult because I only slept about two hours the night before. As I later learned, I was tested after a guy who was pretty much born for riding and easily did around 22-23 mph averages on his light days; when the lab crew was hit with the contrast, they decided

Confessions of an Ironman

to cut the bike portion of my assessment short so that I wouldn't fall off the machine and die. The results of the test confirmed that my biking had quite a bit of room for improvement with respect to both strength and technique, but my running on the treadmill was all right. On the treadmill, when I asked the lab assistants how much longer I should keep running, since it seemed to me that I had been running at a pretty high intensity for quite some time, their answer was, "Oh, we've been done for a while now, actually, but some people prefer to push it all the way until they collapse up there." I, for one, certainly did not belong to that apparently sizable group and immediately hit the red shut-off button, not hiding my resentment that they hadn't stopped me sooner. The purpose of this performance diagnostics test was to help the coach set individual target heart rate zones for each athlete in which our various trainings were to be done later.

In that same week, we tackled the usual 400m swim time trial and I also stumbled upon my very first 3000-meter (about 3300 yards) running time trial. Right before the latter, I asked Ákos what tactics one should approach that distance with, as I had never gauged myself for anything like that before and had no clue as to what pace I ought to target. I thought I had to be able to stack three 4-minute kilometers (6:26 per mile pace) somehow, but when I told Ákos, all he said was that it might be a tad ambitious for the time being. I ended up with a time of 12-minutes 4 seconds, despite my long break due to the vacation, and I was absolutely satisfied with that.

The monotony of my comfortable rides at home was also broken by certain new exercises that were gradually introduced, such as one-legged pedaling or pushing the highest gear for strength training. The latter I had no problems with whatsoever, as it used to be my standard gear setting, but when I first attempted the exercise under the code name "4x2-minute one-legged spin" right in front of my TV set, it didn't take longer than about 8-10 seconds before I started squeezing the handlebars with my eyes fixated on the timer. At that time, I still couldn't execute the correct technique using the

In Case I Got Used to It ...

SPD pedals and I also had my work cut out on the strength-training front.

Just before the end of the year, right around Christmas, I put in an easy run in Jészberény, my hometown. On December 26th I was back to my "favorite" course on Gellért Hill, not real y having to fight any crowds. I must admit, I actually liked training in extreme conditions, which most people prefer to avoid, because when I was out there, almost entirely alone, hardly seeing any (crazy?) people with similar determination to mine, my accomplishment gave me even greater satisfaction. Extreme conditions weren't sparse in winter. For example, in January, at the beginning of the third training cycle, I attempted to complete my hill run on ice-covered roads. This exercise ended up being more of a survival game, the whole time trying to avoid getting injured by hitting the pavement. When I think about these sessions, I realize that each and every one are unforgettable experiences. One time, when it was more about negotiating the ice than running, there was a car coming from the opposite direction as I was running down hill and I noticed that the driver's eyes – he was an elderly gentleman – were fixated on me. I didn't think it would be a good idea to get into any conflict, so I made sure to pull way over to the side. The guy still slowed down, almost coming to a stop, and he even had his window down by the time I came up next to him. I was pleasantly surprised when, instead of screaming obscenities, he said, "Your will is admirable." His remark lifted my spirits immensely.

I have never lacked the necessary will when in pursuit of any of my goals. In amateur sports the path is not especially difficult; if you ask for expert help, you will inevitably be set in the right direction, told to do the right things, and make the necessary improvements that will enable you to reach your goal. Your part in that equation is "simply" to execute what you are told to do after asking for proper help. I waited too long to do that. Not that I would have been able to do the full distance any earlier even if I had had help, but I would have certainly spared myself a lot of suffering and disappointment. If I were to do it again, I would do it differently, without a doubt,

Confessions of an Ironman

especially after hearing Ákos' lecture on training theories, where it became crystal clear that the science behind the training was very complex. While I knew that training was a field of study in itself, I was also sure that I was not interested enough to dig into it. For me, the most obvious solution was to go out and "purchase" the product of this knowledge (a carefully crafted training plan) that was especially designed to suit my needs, along with the constant supervision, which ensured that I was headed in the right direction. Why reinvent the wheel when it was readily available?

I have had seemingly unattainable goals in other areas of my life. However, I wasn't always fortunate enough to acquire credible, expert help, which might have speeded up my progress and kept me on the right track to success. To find an example, I don't have to go further than my childhood dream of realizing financial freedom.

It was very motivating that, as a result of the accurate execution of my training plan, I was getting stronger and faster, which I not only felt but was able to measure. I could always use that positive feedback to convince myself to tackle what was prescribed for any given day. It was never really a question whether I'd actually do the work required, but the truth is, I liked feeling sorry for myself from time to time. At the end of January, I clocked 11 minutes 39 seconds in the running time trial, which I felt was a commendable improvement compared to my previous level.

These assessments usually fell on the rest weeks, which should be regarded as "somewhat lighter" weeks. Although I knew that it wasn't the best idea to shuffle around the individual elements of my training plan, since the various training sessions were deliberately placed on a given day allowing the necessary time to pass between each specific workload, I still ventured into moving the Saturday hill run to Friday during the easier weeks of some of the cycles, and did them after the morning swim, to free up an extra day for myself so that I could go home to Jászberény. It was my little brother who missed me the most – or so I was told – and at that stage of the training plan, I could still make the trip home every once in a while. (Later, my weekends became filled with seemingly endless bike rides, followed by long runs the next day and many hours of sleep, which proved to be a superb and much needed complement to both.)

Until You Can Learn to Love Yourself...

I could write a whole book about what I learned regarding those in my immediate and wider circles, but I have decided to limit my thoughts so that I can keep most of my friends.

It was illuminating to see who those people were that stood behind me and were genuinely happy about my development, and to recognize those who felt that they were somehow made less by my progress. Those in the latter group – perhaps unknowingly – regularly made some pretty piercing remarks. I came to realize that only those people who are satisfied with their own lives are capable of applauding the success of others. It is amazing how true the principle is which says that you can only love others to the extent that you love yourself, which is why those that are not "okay with themselves" are unable to give real love. There is a very good reason why we hear the following announcement at the beginning of every flight: "...In the unlikely event of a sudden loss of cabin pressure, secure your own oxygen mask before helping others!" Taking care of your things first is not selfish at all, because that is the only way you can make other things work, too. It is the natural order.

The growth of my own self-respect increased the quality of my relationships; I believe the parallel between the two is no coincidence.

IT FEELS LIKE IT IS
TIME FOR A MARATHON

By the end of February, having done no races since the less than pleasant Budapest Marathon, I thought it would be a good idea to run the Barcelona Marathon in March. I didn't have any specific goals for the race, I was just interested in it for the sake of adventure.

I told Ákos all about my fantastic idea on a Monday, during our gym session. His answer was simply that it was way too early for that. I didn't know what to say since I was convinced that I could run a marathon any time. It didn't matter to me that there was much less running in my training plan then, compared to what I had done on my own before. I still felt that it would be just fine. Nonetheless, I didn't push it, and gave up on Barcelona for the time being.

Training week after week without races to compete in became a little boring. I guess this is what sparks a very common mistake that many amateurs tend to make. Namely, they make ad hoc race decisions, inserting unplanned items into their training plans, which end up hindering their own development. Truth be told, I never knew what the science behind my training plan was but I still went and did it anyway, knowing nothing about the underlying principles. I attended a sports science presentation after the Ironman,[10] as I

---

[10] There weren't any events like that organized by the club before.

It Feels Like It Is Time for a Marathon

figured I should at least know the basics before writing this book. Despite that, I still do not consider myself an expert on the subject. My story is not meant to address the scientific theories of training; the best way to learn about those are to find the experts who have devoted their lives to the discipline.

The first week of the fourth training cycle, which fell right around the beginning of February, 2016, was memorable for all the wrong reasons. I had developed a fever and could hardly eat. I rarely got sick but instead might feel weaker than usual for one or two days a year. Consequently, I didn't really know how to handle the situation. I went on with my training as usual. At the Tuesday swim, we were to do a 30x66 meter set (about 70 yards), among other things, and when I went to do my very last flip turn, my right calf cramped up. Nothing like that had happened to me before and I had no idea what I was supposed to do about it, how long the pain would last, or how it could have been prevented. I went to running practice that evening (with a fever, as it turned out) – but at least that session served as an opportunity to learn from one of my teammates, who happened to be a doctor, that based on my level of training it wouldn't be a bad idea to supplement my diet with calcium and magnesium, not forgetting some essential minerals, either. My knowledge of these supplements was as limited as my understanding of what a nutrition plan was, although with race day nearing and the workloads steadily growing, it was high time I started familiarizing myself with that info as well.

It was in the middle of my "sick week" that a new task was introduced for my Saturday runs – a little twist, just to add some discomfort. The Saturday prescription now included "a 75-minute run on hilly terrain, with 10x1-minute hill repeats. Try to pick a moderately steep hill! The jog down is the rest." As difficult as the task felt in the beginning, I progressed quickly and acclimated to the new routine.

Confessions of an Ironman

The *Dragon Ball* Success Recipe

When I was in high school there was a manga animation series on TV called *Dragon Ball*. I almost always watched in the afternoons because it was a lot of fun, plus it was a great way to put off studying. The main character, Son Goku, seemed to believe in "extreme training conditions." He wore heavy armor to fly around, to fight, and to work out. When he was faced with difficult battles and got rid of the massive gear that slowed him down, he surprised even himself by how quickly he could move, how much stronger the training had made him, and realized that beating his opponents was not even a true challenge anymore.

I thought about this cartoon a lot while suffering in the pool with my ankles tied together or while wearing other "equipment" that made training feel more like torture. Having to experience these difficulties, however, made my mind feel more at ease and the challenges ahead seemed greatly diminished. I knew that during any race I could actually use both my arms and legs for the swim with no restrictions on breathing, either. I wouldn't be "tied up" in the water and I could utilize all my gears on the bike, not to mention that the running course was almost always completely flat. Training sessions spiced up with various torture-like tools worked wonders because they could make the race feel more like a celebration instead of a challenge.

THE SECOND SHOCK

At the end of February, I started to feel sorry for myself again. I had two weekly bike sessions, one was two hours long and the other was two and a half hours, and I still didn't like sitting on that thing. All other workloads were increasing as well, but I didn't mind. For instance, my runs grew in length by 10 minutes here and there, but because my running was at a completely different level, I actually enjoyed being challenged with more difficult assignments in that discipline.

The scheduled time trials revealed that my swimming had improved somewhat, but the interval sessions had not had the same positive effects on my running. I was not getting better being stuck between the best runners in the club and the rest; I couldn't quite keep up with the 3-4 fastest guys, yet I was usually faster than all the others. I ended up running alone and my time had not changed from the previous measure of 11:39.

I continued with two bike rides per week until the end of March, which meant about 5 hours in the saddle, spiced up with various exercises. It was around then that I noticed my back was not killing me anymore while pedaling. I had bad posture to start with, which didn't quite give me an edge in sports. Additionally, my technique was most certainly poor; it was likely that my bike set up was also far from optimal, and I was weak, too. But, besides all that – or perhaps as a direct result of it – another reason I dreaded biking was that roughly 30 minutes into each session, I ended up in serious pain.

Confessions of an Ironman

The more experienced athletes didn't make a big deal out of that, and simply said there was nothing I could do but give it time and I'd get used to it. (This remains my biggest problem with triathlon – I just cannot make peace with the "you'll get used to it" approach on the bike – so I only kept at it until it was absolutely necessary in order to reach my goal.) March was the first month I mentioned to Ákos in my weekly feedback that my back had not been hurting during my rides as much as before. I was certain that this positive change also had to do with all the core strengthening work I had been doing during the Monday gym sessions and on my own, on Saturdays.

The March training cycle was more about pushing the run as far as possible, and the serious bike sessions had to wait. Toward the end of the month, my Saturday hill run quota had grown to 105 minutes with 14x1-minute hill repeats. I remember when I was right around that part of the session, I glanced at my watch and registered that I had "only 40 minutes left." Only 40 minutes? My very first Gellért Hill run flashed before my eyes, where 40 minutes nearly made up the entire session. What an immense struggle it had been to make it through! It was an incredible feeling to realize how far I had come in roughly four months' time. It seemed an unmistakable piece of evidence that I should have asked for professional help much sooner.

I also started noticing the positive effects of all those low heart rate sessions, which I previously believed to be utterly useless, being as incompetent as I was. Initially, it annoyed the hell out of me that I was only able to clock slower than 9:40-minute miles in order to keep my heart rate within the required limits, which felt more like crawling than anything else. By the time March rolled around, though, I was able to maintain sub 9:40-minute miles even during these easy, low heart rate runs, too. This type of progress is a very important milestone in endurance sports!

Before the start of April, the following sentence left Ákos' mouth (which put me at unease immediately, even though I did not know

The Second Shock

what it meant): "Starting from the next cycle, we'll begin to take the bike seriously." As far I was concerned, the 5 hours a week biking assignments seemed plenty serious, especially with all those added, extra special heart rate-based task variations that were inserted in my 3-hour session, making my living room a site of never-before-seen struggles.

It was around this time that Robi, one of the guys who was preparing with me, raised the question of how it would be possible to make the recovery between training sessions quicker and more effective. We were nearing 13-hour training weeks and it was not easy to bring ourselves to an optimal state, to be adequately rested before each practice. We put our heads together after a freezing cold interval session and Ákos made some adjustments to our weekly schedules to optimize them to our new and not very forgiving training plan, which was to begin in April. He also told each of us individually which products he recommended that could help with recovery, what we could use for refueling while training, and what other things we ought to try before the race.

Once again, I received new and very useful information. Then, and still today, I have mixed feelings about this topic: On the one hand, I am not willing to load my body with all kinds of chemical waste just to shave a few minutes off my time in a race. On the other hand, I was fully aware I would not be able to do all that work set out for me if I didn't make a conscious effort to replenish what my body used up during some of the more demanding training sessions. I took some notes, and after doing some research on the web, I went through the list to see what I was willing to use.

Ákos' recommendations were certainly great, but I was not the usual training subject. My diet at the time almost completely excluded animal products, so the standard line up of protein supplements or "recovery shakes" had to be ruled out. To make things more difficult, I am lactose intolerant, and nothing stays in me that contains lactose. I am being very diplomatic when describing this problem, believe me.

Confessions of an Ironman

Here is the menu I settled on in the end: I always carried rice protein with me for the Monday gym sessions. There are some who day in day out guzzle that stuff, even if they move a pinky, because they think they'll be quicker to grow muscle. I did not have that sort of aspiration, and I only drank it after workouts that involved the TRX bands. (And maybe later, during the last phases of preparation, after the 5-6-hour bike rides. I didn't think twice about what I ate or drank then; I consumed everything I could get my hands on at home.) Ákos recommended that I also try some mineral supplements in powder form, along with carnitine. Different things work for different people, but what seemed to do me justice was a carnitine drink before the long sessions, followed by a mineral drink afterwards. I did not use any other "magic potion" or super product to enhance my performance.

I drank isotonic drinks and water during my long rides, plus I experimented with a wide range of energy bars and gels. Starting out, I didn't feel inclined to think about nutrition while training, but the training plan and my energy levels soon made me realize that I didn't have much of a choice; the time for testing these things had arrived.

IT WAS NOT AN APRIL FOOL'S DAY JOKE, UNFORTUNATELY

When I glimpsed the first week of the sixth training cycle, which was to start in April, I seriously considered the possibility that I might be mad. The weekly training hours total had risen to 16 and 4 bike rides were included. My Tuesdays, from that point on, included a bike session after swimming, which I was to follow with a run right off the bike to ensure I had a combined workout. In actuality, this meant my entire morning was filled, not to mention that I had plenty of time to test those energy bars as I was practically living on them until the early afternoon. Besides that, I thought my Saturdays also gave my life a highly enviable twist, with an hour-and-a-half bike ride coupled with a mountain run of the same duration. Still, one could argue that the Sunday 2.5-hour bike followed by an hour

The Second Shock

run was not too shabby, either. On top of that, both days included exercises that were to be executed in specific heart rate zones and at specific tempos.

Just when I had gotten used to my current training load, there it was, the next "act." This would take time to get used to. It was time again for more suffering and self-pity; nonetheless, my goal remained clear, nothing could change it.

Not that there was any need for additional challenges, but taking my bike off the home trainer as the weather started to shift for the better was a sizable contrast, to say the least. I was outside again, and it felt like I was in a different dimension. What I had done indoors seemed completely different. I felt weak and could barely complete my assignments. The feedback I sent to Ákos for a few weeks was usually along these lines: "The best thing I can say about this session is that I have finished it but the actual content didn't have a whole lot to do with the original assignment." That bothered me a lot, because the season was upon me, my time was running out, and I did not feel prepared at all.

IT STARTED OUT AS A REWARD MARATHON

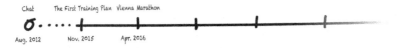

After having been forced to ditch the idea of the Barcelona Marathon, I somehow managed to work the Vienna City Marathon into my training plan. It was exciting, because I was pretty sure I could break my personal best with all the Ironman preparation I had under my belt. It also gave me a legitimate excuse to miss some of my bike training. I did not have a special plan for the race, all I wanted was to keep my pace near 8 minutes per mile.

The shortest and most concise way to summarize this adventure is to quote what I wrote Ákos in my weekly summary: "I still have not learned to run smart, which makes these things very painful." It just so happened that I started out around a 7:40 per mile pace (which was so near 8:00, that it made no difference really - or at least that's what I thought at the time), and got completely spent by mile 19. It wasn't like my most recent screw-up in the Budapest Marathon – here I had serious doubts that I could even finish the race. My pace slowed to outside 9:40 miles, which, as slow as it is, still can't describe what I went through to reach the finish line. I clocked 3 hours and 38 minutes, and I was very unhappy about it. I kept thinking that if I couldn't even do a marathon properly – how was I going to do an Ironman?!

Naturally, I was at the gym the next day for our usual strength training session, which was part of my 16.5-hour weekly training plan. It was a nice way to get my thighs "loosened up." Ákos' opinion of my weekend performance was much different from mine. The way he saw it, I only missed my personal best by a mere two minutes, while being in the thick of a demanding training regimen

The Second Shock

and tired from a high workload. Had it not turned out like that, and I quote, 'we'd be doing something very wrong." Simply put, it was alright that I ran my tanks empty by the 19th mile, doing it off of hard training, having not let up one bit before to rest – not to mention, that I went out way too fast again, because the 8 minutes per mile pace is not 7:40!

There was, however, another finisher medal. This one was shaped like a star. I needed to survive one more week before my "rest" period, where I could get myself together again. Looking back, I can see that forcing this marathon into my training plan had not been a very good idea after all.

The fact of the matter is that the timing of my little "run out" could not have been worse. It coincided with a training cycle where we even left out the time trials because, as Ákos said, increased mileage on the bike always causes the running performance to suffer. The wise thing, therefore, was to avoid hurting our self-confidence with those more than likely unattractive running times. I had decided to do a marathon instead, which ended up being just as detrimental. It was my fifth official marathon, but I had yet to do one running smart, with the right pacing.

Self-Confidence is Fragile, while Self-Esteem is Long Lasting

Many people use self-confidence and self-esteem interchangeably just as I did until I heard a lecture from Tibor Kerner, a life, business, and executive coach. He shed light on the enormous difference between the two terms. Self-confidence is gained through external input from the environment, in the forms of feedback and results, whereas self-esteem is sparked from within: It is a feeling that we are indeed good enough and valuable just as we are, regardless of any outside factors.

Confessions of an Ironman

> Success (whatever that may be – money, existential position, a sports title, etc.) will only amplify what IS ALREADY THERE. Consequently, people with low self-esteem – who do not believe that they are valuable individuals – are unable to genuinely enjoy success because they don't feel they deserve it. (Also known as impostor syndrome.) If you feel that you don't deserve something, it will inevitably lead to losing it, and the absence of success reflected from the outside will result in a breakdown.
>
> Only an innate self-esteem can be long lasting; that is what one should nurture. Self-confidence that is fueled by outside success is always going to be unstable, and thus inescapably leads to collapse.

I HAD BEEN AVOIDING GROUP RIDES

I would like to disclose as objectively as possible, without labeling myself in any way, that I tend to think of myself as the lowest performer in a given group. Let's just say that if I sat down with someone who told me that he or she runs marathons, I would naturally think that this person was a better runner. (There are countless examples I could list from other areas of my life. I am aware of this tendency and try to consciously manage it.)

> ### Self-Image vs. Reality
>
> I remember, I was home, sitting at my desk, hovering over a blank piece of paper with a pencil in my hand. No, I wasn't about to put my unparalleled drawing skills into action. Rather, I was trying to figure out what time splits would ensure I didn't come in dead last at the Ironman 70.3 Budapest. That was the only goal I felt I could feasibly shoot for when planning that race. I

The Second Shock

opened a PDF that listed the previous year's results, and began my calculations to come up with the times for the swim, the bike, and the run to save myself from complete embarrassment.

My way of thinking was rooted in my childhood. I recall being marked as a clumsy kid, so I quickly defaulted to an "I cannot win" attitude. From that point on, instead of trying to win, my approach was always to avoid getting beaten. (For example, I didn't like to play soccer when we kept score. Instead, I just liked to play for the heck of it, ruling out any chances of losing.) The difference in approach is profound, similarly to its consequences, until its roots are exposed, enabling the individual to begin working on their issue.

What you think about yourself is extremely important, even if that self-image is rooted in an unrealistic foundation. **Any difference between your self-image and reality can only exist temporarily.** Reread that sentence as many times as necessary to understand its significance and to realize that the only way to lead an authentic life is by working on yourself, improving your self-image and, as a result, building your new reality.

These thoughts lingered in the back of my mind each time my teammates invited me to join them for the weekend rides together. Those long sessions would surely be more enjoyable if we could help one another fight through them. I never felt good enough, however, so I was quite relieved when I was able to skip these events on the few occasions there were scheduling conflicts. Later, even Ákos made it a point to remind me that it would be a good idea to join the others for those long weekend rides. He felt that I could greatly benefit from that new stimulus.

On Saturday, April 30, we agreed to meet in the morning for a 3-hour ride together. The session was part of my prescribed training plan. Although the assignment also specified a low heart rate session,

Confessions of an Ironman

not more than a few hundred meters into the ride I quickly had to regard that requirement as optional if I wanted to keep up with the boys. There it was, the "new stimulus." As Ákos noted, it could be greatly beneficial. There were four of us: Robi, who made going uphill look like child's play, Peti, who was on his bike pretty much all the time, and then Ervin and I, the two left fighting for our lives. We picked the Szentendre – Visegrád route (two small towns north of Budapest), which meant nothing to me as I had only ridden one route before, toward Fót, all by myself. I'll never forget that we had just barely passed the city limits when I was already looking at my watch to see how much longer we had left; I was already short of breath. The road was mostly flat, until we got to Visegrád, where I got a glimpse of a sign with the worrisome name "Cloud Castle." I was convinced we'd be headed in a different direction, but those who felt comfortable in the saddle thought differently. It turned out that we climbed to Paprét (Priests' Meadow), as I was later told by those who actually knew the area. Whenever I am faced with any difficult challenges in training, my approach is to always try to get it over with as quickly as possible, so I did my best to get a move on up the hill. My attitude got me a respectable "podium finish" because our little group got broken up quite a bit during the climb, and we decided that we'd wait for one another at the summit. Robi, who disappeared pretty much after the first turn going up, only admitted once we were all at the top that he had "a significant cycling history." My mind was racing, looking at the situation I had managed to put myself in again. We had only gotten halfway through the ride and I needed to gather myself so that I could make it back with the pack.

On the bright side, it was a great opportunity to test the energy bars and the gels. These were clearly needed to ensure my survival. The Garmin statistics revealed that we managed to include a 30-minute climbing section into an otherwise extremely challenging project with 1312 feet of elevation gain. I am fairly sure that the 19% of

The Second Shock

time spent in the 3-hour bike ride in the actual target zone, the 47% in the so-called manageable zone, and the 34% in the borderline death zone paints an accurate picture of how I felt about that whole adventure. Since the latter 34% amounted to a full hour of highly exerting work, I was pretty much over and done with by the time I got home. I was immediately supposed to head out for an hour of running spiced up with various tasks, in specific heart rate target zones. That took a lot of determination to accomplish, I have to admit.

Joining with the others for the ride was a good thing. It forced me out of my comfort zone, as I had to struggle to keep up with them. If I hadn't kept up, I would not have been able to find my way back into town. (Back when I was a teenager, I had similar motivations while running the 5-milers we were sent out to do during karate practice. I didn't want to be left alone with all those dogs barking in the dark.)

The group ride adventure was beneficial for me in many ways and it served my development well. Despite that, it was still a big leap for me. If I had had a choice, I would not have participated in anything like that again. But the truth is, I had no choice. The race was nearing and I still had progress to make. Robi could not make it for the other rides that followed, so the pace became more manageable. This ended up being the target of numerous jokes during our morning swims.

This was also a time when I successfully battled my greatest cycling nemesis, the tire change. I frequently had to switch my bike from the indoor trainer set up – which I always reverted back to when the weather turned rainy – to the outdoor configuration. This meant countless changes from the blue Tacx tire that was supplied with the home trainer, to the Maxxis Detonator which my bike originally came with.

Confessions of an Ironman

I had previously considered the removal of the rear wheel an extra-tricky maneuver. Becoming well practiced in that skill gave me quite a bit of added self-confidence. Looking at the number of oily spots on my living room floor and the time it took me to complete the maneuver might not support my argument, but the outcome was always a working bike.

THERE WILL NEVER BE A BETTER CHANCE TO GIVE UP!

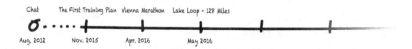

I was still far from believing that I could actually complete the bike leg of the Ironman, let alone do it at around "little better than 19 mph" as Ákos envisioned for me. I am the type of "athlete" who needs tangible proof before an event that he can cover the given distance without major problems. Is it any wonder that I ran a full marathon by the creek, multiple times, on my own?

Seldom would someone attempt an entire Ironman as training, but there was no question in my mind that I needed to complete the bike portion on its own. When I found an ad on Facebook promoting a ride around Lake Balaton, a 128-mile cycling event that was not a race but a sporting event with the aim of doing a loop around the lake, I was certain it was just the thing for me! All I wanted was to complete the ride at a comfortable pace and – not surprisingly – collect the finisher medal. My plan seemed perfect up until Robi decided to join in, suggesting that we should roll together. Coming off of our Visegrád adventure, I had serious doubts that I could actually keep up with him over the longest ride of my life. We made plans to start out together and I would fall back if needed. Getting

Confessions of an Ironman

lost was out of the question in such a pack and I could easily join up with others on the road if I so desired.

This ingenious idea was included in my 19-hour plus training week record for a Saturday, under the code name "Lake Loop – 128 miles," I was to follow the loop with a 16-mile easy "cooldown" run on Sunday. (If you are ever looking for a full weekend program, spiels of this sort can easily get you booked up with their connected eating and sleeping "sessions.")

After completing the first five days of the training week, we arrived at Balatonföldvár, the town where the event would start. The weather did not seem promising. The owner of our little hotel even remarked that he did not understand why so many people turned out for the event each year because they always had to ride in the rain. That was music to my ears, since there were two things I had not done before – ride in the rain and spend enough time in the saddle to bike 128 miles. The next morning, I learned that I was going to get a chance to do both. I would also experience firsthand why real cyclists do not recommend riding narrow-tired bikes on wet roads. It was pouring and extremely cold. As I recall, I wore a base layer, a long-sleeve mid layer, a windbreaker, a scarf, and one more vest over it all.

Robi was with a few friends of his, so after the start we arranged ourselves in a pack. They took the front, and I followed. It didn't come as a surprise that the first few miles were about their search for the lead and not about finding the comfortable pace for which I had originally planned. In case it is not evident by this point, it was not only speed and endurance that I lacked, but I had quite a bit of room for improvement in my bike handling skills, too. Maneuvering in the pack also presented me with considerable challenges. Then something unexpected happened: One of Robi's friends got a flat early in the ride. There we were, standing in the cold, pouring rain, while this guy jumped the fence of a nearby kindergarten to find cover where he could change his inner tube. It took him multiple attempts before he realized his efforts were in vain; the outer tire

There Will Never Be a Better Chance to Give Up!

had been so damaged when he slipped that a replaced inner tube would only get ruined again. We called the organizers for help, but Robi and I did not wait for their arrival. We got back on the road. Robi told me one of the guys left behind was not much of a rider, so he would not have been able to keep up with us until the end anyways. I couldn't help but think that perhaps his slower pace could have made my survival a little less precarious as we relentlessly pushed on at a seemingly suicidal speed, cutting through an endless curtain of rain on extremely slippery roads.

Every once in a while we received warning signals that we should take it a little easier, but we kept pushing on, disregarding all of them. I don't think Robi would take offence if I said that he is a fanatic when it comes to these sorts of challenges, and I am the type who does not like to lag behind anyone and tends to push himself beyond what is reasonable. I exerted myself way over my limits once again. My chances of survival were amplified by the fact that Robi could not quite dictate his usual, merciless pace on the crowded and very slippery roads, but even with those limitations, we were still among the fastest there. At times, we had some distance between us, and it was during one of those separations when I thought our team ride was over, that I would not be able to make it up to his wheel again. But then one more ray of hope appeared because Robi's bike slipped from under him as he crossed a wooden bridge and he hit the ground in a spectacular manner. My first thought was I hoped he was all right, and he did jump up after the fall; but I was also glad that I got yet another chance to catch up to him. Just as these thoughts were running through my head, I found myself right where he fell and copied his move with near 100% accuracy. I ate the ground big-time, banged up my elbow really hard, but my bike was intact and we could carry on.

I don't recall that any of what happened altered our approach to the ride; we kept on without any added caution to our "stride," biking at the same speed as before. For Robi, this pace was the usual warm-up tempo. I didn't hold back because 128 miles seemed like a very

Confessions of an Ironman

long way to go; I felt that if I did it any slower, the torturous ride would never come to an end in those grim conditions.

I was always glad when we approached an aid station. We took a little time to stop at some of them and I got a chance to gather myself. When seeing our triathlon vests, many people concluded that we might be serious cyclists – which was way wrong in my case, of course – so every now and again we were joined by other riders who tried to keep up with us. Every time a group like that decided that our pace was a bit more than what they were cut out for, a new pack of candidates took their place. It wasn't only myself staring at Robi's back for long miles, there were many others as well.

Right round mile 56, we got to the least ideal rainy terrain, some cobblestone-covered roads. Robi, sticking to his usual ways, did not slow down much, but he didn't come out of the situation as well as before. He slipped, and as his bike hit the stones, his rear derailleur broke off. At that point, we had only one "follower" who had been able to keep up the pace. From then on, after two short minutes of damage assessment, we had to conclude that Robi's ride was definitely over. His bike was beyond any repair that could have been done on the spot. He called the organizers to pick him up, and I got back in the saddle and continued on with the stranger.

We slowed to a somewhat more cautious speed, but I lost my shadow fairly quickly as my cycling buddy decided at the next aid station that he would not continue. (Many riders gave up that day because of the relentless and also very dangerous weather. As a result, the sports adventure value of the event quickly disintegrated to near-zero, not to mention the level of how enjoyable the circumstances made the whole experience – if one could actually regard a 128-mile bike ride enjoyable.) I was alone. I saw some families, doing about 12 miles an hour, but I felt I couldn't join them. I was on a training ride after all, and those who were faster had long been gone. I was not familiar with the course, which, at certain places was very poorly marked, and I had no idea how to approach the remaining 68 miles so that I could actually survive.

There Will Never Be a Better Chance to Give Up!

It was around halfway when the realization hit me that I was very wrong in my approach to the whole ride. The bike roads on the north side of Lake Balaton were completely covered in water, making them totally invisible. Using the brakes was pointless: There was one spot where I didn't realize that the bike path crossed the main road, where it would have been advisable at least to slow down, let alone stop. Naturally, I pulled on the brakes as hard as I could, so I only crossed the road (without stopping!) at 15.5 instead of 19 mph. To my great luck, there were no cars coming. It was beyond frightening. I knew that I had to let go of my time expectation or any similar aspirations, otherwise I could end up in big trouble. But still, I could not let go of my ego entirely. The next warning was even more serious.

I was negotiating a downhill section, complete with twists and turns, when, despite my efforts to slow down, my bike gained momentum. The real problem was that the standing water at the bottom of the road completely covered the pavement and I did not see that the bike path took a sudden right turn. I did not stand a chance to make that turn! I hit the brakes as firmly as I could, but my bike, seemingly without a change in speed, kept on going. I jerked my handlebar to the side and the next thing I heard was a huge bang as my bike and helmet hit a metal rail. The next thing I remember is lying on the ground under the guard rail with my bike next to me, soaking wet, and too frightened to move a muscle. The guy ahead of me must have heard the crash because he shouted back: "Couldn't make the turn?" He came back to try and help me. We agreed it would not be a good idea to move me so as not to possibly make things worse, but he tried to fix the brake and derailleur parts on my bike, that looked to be in bad shape, so that I could keep going in case I was able to collect myself.

Meanwhile, many riders caught up with us, giving me and my poor "close out sale" Merida some pretty interesting looks. While this was happening, I realized that although my helmet probably saved my life, I had still banged my noggin badly. I kept thinking that I could have all kinds of injuries that were not visible at first glance

Confessions of an Ironman

and getting back on the bike for 62 more miles would not be a very smart idea. Another argument raged in my head: "I am not the type who gives up. If I carry on, the miles will hopefully tick away faster than my life." I made a pact with myself to go on, but strictly in touring mode, switching back to a much slower speed. If I felt any serious discomfort, I would immediately stop and ask for help.

The rest of the ride was "pleasant." I had another chance to taste the wooden bridge. This time a different guy, without a helmet – or hair – crashed very badly in front of me, hitting the ground head first. Everything was covered in blood and I had to do an emergency braking maneuver on the slippery wood to avoid going right over his motionless body. A few of us stopped to help him. Later, on a very steep uphill, I learned that my front derailleur was broken. I actually had to get off the bike and, while holding the loose brake lever in place with one hand, I was trying to shift with the other. Those passing me clearly had some quality entertainment.

The lake loop really had it all: High speed riding, a near-death experience, I had to be assisted, and I also assisted others. Interestingly, my biggest fear, which was whether my legs would hold up, hardly crossed my mind. With all that time on my hands, I even had a chance to test each of my different sports foods.

I couldn't wrap my head around how much self-hatred I must be laden with if I was willing to expose myself to such crazy punishment. This latest biking experiment could have easily ended up being fatal. What else needed to happen for me to finally learn the lesson? It might be time to give up the whole thing. On the other side of the scale, with more weight than any common sense could bear, was my "I don't give up" attitude. Having made a commitment to a goal, and being well on the road to accomplishing it, I'd rather perish than give up.

WHY?

There is a fine line between healthy perseverance and irrational stubbornness. I still have a lot to learn to effectively navigate between the two.

I've come across a story a few times about two trees. One tree is rigid, standing firm against the elements, while the other is supple, twisting and turning in harmony with the wind. Formidable storms will break the stiff tree sooner or later, but its agile mate stands a better chance of survival, even in the most severe circumstances. My concern about this fable is that if people become overly flexible, they may give up at the very first gust of wind, surrendering their goals as soon as they encounter the very first hurdle. With an attitude like that, not a whole lot can be achieved in life. It is not easy to find the ideal middle ground.

It is my experience that life will throw numerous curveballs while one is on a path to achieve great goals. Challenges can serve as excuses to give up, therefore the real question – and perhaps the only question – is whether you have a strong enough WHY? What is your motivation behind your goal? Why are you doing what you are doing? How committed are you? The answers to these questions will be the determining factors when you come to a crossroads – which you certainly will – and when you have to decide whether you will continue with your quest or begin searching for a new goal. Make no mistake; it may seem easy to justify your change of path any time a "redirected goal chase" happens, but the reality is that every one of your half-finished attempts to reach a goal will erode your self-respect, eventually making you incapable of accomplishing anything. Even the most mundane of things.

Looking at two seemingly unreachable goals from my life as examples – attaining financial freedom and completing an

Confessions of an Ironman

Ironman – it is very easy to find the parallels. I had very strong underlying motivations in both cases; rock solid WHYs stood behind me, making it practically impossible for me to abandon my goals before the finish line. These WHYs were much needed, too, countless times along the way!

Constructive and positive WHYs are very important. While it may not seem crucial for the sake of reaching a given goal, it is extremely important for the sake of your future. You can make things happen out of malice or sheer stubbornness, but the feeling of success will be totally different when it stems from healthy motivation.

If you are like me and refuse to quit even when faced with great hurdles, then you may go on to achieve fantastic goals. I recommend you take the time to examine your underlying motivations first, going deep to uncover why a given goal is important to you. Had I seen the WHYs behind my Ironman, or had there been anyone to shed light on them while I was still in the planning phase, it is highly likely I would not have kept on with my pursuit. For some reason, that journey was the way through which I could come to all my priceless realizations. Being at the level of consciousness where I was then, I could not have made a different decision, and I fully accept that.

As my preparations progressed and I began to uncover my underlying motivations, I was not happy about the things I discovered. But since I had already made my commitment, I was certain beyond any doubt that I would complete the project and I would learn everything I could from the experience. If you are the kind of person who is unable to leave things incomplete, it is important you take the time when defining your goals to dig deep into your WHYs.

At the aid stations, I made sure I took as much on board as possible, and then I kept on rolling towards the finish line. I cannot say that

There Will Never Be a Better Chance to Give Up!

the tempo was safe. I don't know if there would have been such a thing on those wet roads. I am simply unfit to hold myself back, so the built-in alarm that went off from time to time, reminding me that "hey, I couldn't have stopped here, even if I wanted to," proved to be very useful. Like when I slipped into the opposite lane in a tunnel and only missed a concrete wall by about 1 or 2 inches. The end of the day could not come soon enough. Anikó and Robi were waiting for me at the finish, and were very happy to see me arrive in one piece. Earlier that day, it crossed my mind that it would be a great Ironman training if I quickly changed out after the ride and did the 16-mile Sunday run right after 128 miles in the saddle. Once the ride was done, however, it did not take much to convince myself of the opposite. I was happy that I survived the adventure, and I had a lot to think about.

During the Sunday run – the next day, as scheduled – I had plenty of time to ponder what I had gained from the extreme cycling day. Although my tempo was still not quite where it needed to be, I was reassured that all the work I had put into my trainings was not in vain and I was capable of going the distance. It was also clear that I could keep down those energy bars and gels over longer distances, which was more than encouraging in light of what was to come. This adventure gave my self-confidence an enormous boost, and the fact that I had not given up despite the adverse conditions crystalized my belief that there wasn't anything that could prevent me from completing the Ironman. (Truth is, my feeling of certainty was a bit early; I didn't have to wait long before "anything" actually came along.)

On Sunday, as usual, I sent Ákos my weekly training data along with a few feedback thoughts. I was joyfully awaiting the next lighter training week. I knew I could use the rest. When the training plan arrived that evening, I quickly learned that "easing up" meant a 12-hour workload with the race in close proximity. When I saw that, I just wanted the whole thing to be over and done with. It seemed my life would not get easier or better until then.

WHAT DOES THE IRONMAN PREPARATION DEMAND FROM A ROOKIE?

Had I not had numerous conversations with my many teammates who were also preparing for the very first Ironman of their lives, I would not dare write about this. I don't think my own example alone would justify any conclusions.

Workloads were increasing to new heights with the nearing of the final stretch of our training. The talks after our team sessions were filled with more and more questions such as "How well are you able to recover? How are you holding up? Can you do your day job with all that training?"

To me, a 20-hour training week looks bad even on paper, and the sheer sight of it on a computer screen makes a hobby athlete ponder. The truth is that the number of hours spent training does not even begin to describe how much sacrifice that final phase of the preparations demand. Let's look at the 20-hour example. First of all, this number relates to net workout hours and does not include the "get there, warm up before, stretch out after" parts. Second, being as oblivious as I was, I never calculated that my body's need for sleep would increase exponentially. (I may happen to be extreme in that regard, meaning I was just fine with 5-6 hours of sleep before, but nearing the end of the preparations, I really needed those 8-9 hours. When I could not get that much, I felt drained and was not the most pleasant person to be around.)

Furthermore, when I was awake but not training, those around me could still easily detect the effects of my little hobby. As a "day job," I edit a monthly investment newsletter and create video seminars, but I realized that I was simply not rested enough for such creative work. It did not make a difference that the work hours were actually there and set aside, I just could not produce quality work that I felt was up to my own standards. I was convinced that there was a problem with me. That thought kept bugging me until the morning one of my teammates told me he had actually put his business on idle, only doing the bare essentials, because he did not have the energy for anything else other than family and the unusual amount of training.

I am well aware there are countless people who undertake Ironman races while balancing family and work. I did not have any children to look after, nor did I have set work hours during my training, so I had it easy in that regard. The point I am trying to make is that I am convinced a simple chart indicating the direction of a weekly training workload will not help a "rookie" accurately estimate how much time and sacrifice a project of this magnitude will actually demand. Even if you have never put similar quantities of work into training before, you can be certain you can reach the necessary level if you follow the directions of a well-designed training plan. But don't be surprised that in doing so, the feedback your body will give you along with its additional needs may be much different than what you are used to (if nothing else, most certainly regarding nutrition and sleep).

It made me happy that I was able to complete my bigger projects about two months before the race. In the finishing stretch, the only way I would have been able to work on them was if I were to compromise on the quality I otherwise strive for, and that would have been unacceptable to me. My advice to a rookie is not to plan anything important for the final months of preparation. Simply "delivering the musts" at home and at work will consume most of your time and energy.

HIBERNATED LIFE AND DERAILED DRESS REHEARSALS

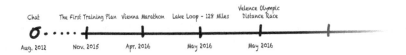

I had a little over two months until the race in Nagyatád. Having hibernated all other areas of my life, it was time to do some triathlons to assess where I stood with my preparations. The first one was a race in Velence at the Olympic distance, a repeat of my very first attempt at the sport with hopes of more success this time.

The race fell on the first week of the eighth training cycle and I can't say we took it into consideration when formulating my workloads: I had 4-hour sessions on both Tuesday and Wednesday. The most delightful session of the week was on Wednesday. My training instructions read: "4 hours of biking including a 6-mile section, steadily increasing the tempo every 1.3 miles, starting from 17-18 mph, accelerating to 21-22 mph. It should be done on relatively flat roads!" Let me just say that flat roads are scarce around Fót, not to mention that the idea of me biking at 21-22 mph still seemed to be in the science fiction category. I didn't let that bother me. I did the 4-hour session, as I did everything else that Ákos had "prescribed."

My heavy training workload meant that my family got pushed to the sidelines quite a bit. I had an idea, which seemed to be a very good one at the time, that I'd "borrow" my little brother for the weekend,

Hibernated Life and Derailed Dress Rehearsals

he'd come to Velence with us to cheer me on and to take a dip in the lake if the weather allowed. The "adventure weekend" began when I asked – or maybe told – Bence to put down the game controller for the Xbox he was playing with and put on a pair of sneakers that he could run in because we were headed outside for a short, easy jog. My home track is about one kilometer (0.6 miles) away from my house, so getting there was no problem. There, I told Bence that I would do a few laps but he could stop any time he felt like it. He was so enthusiastic that after the first 400 meters he was near death. After that, we settled into a pattern where Bence joined me for every other lap, taking a rest in between. It was only later that I learned he much preferred sodas to water, which was strange because he guzzled up my lightly-mixed isotonic drink without a blink of an eye and he didn't even ask what it was. The jog home was more about a test of will (for him) because every time he would stop, announcing that he could not carry on, he got the only answer he could get: "It's too bad because we live a little ways further." He then gathered himself and kept on going. When we finally got home, he immediately called his mom; he was so proud that he ran almost 2 miles.

We didn't make a big deal out of the race in Velence. An Olympic distance triathlon did not make me nervous anymore and we made the trip down on race day. I did not have specific time expectations, I simply wanted to do it for training. The water was cold enough to wear wetsuits for the swim (which didn't bother Bence one bit as he got in the water anyway) but even that couldn't put me at unease. The change in my composure only came after the start signal.

I was in for one of the worst half-hours of my life. In theory, swimming 1500 meters (1640 yards) was not a problem for me; the reality was much different! With so much training under my belt, I expected to do much better, but the same thing happened as the year before. I could not see anything in the water and the entire swim was about getting kicked and punched from every side. Naturally, this immediately triggered my panicking hydrophobia, and from that point on the question was no longer how fast I would

Confessions of an Ironman

complete that ridiculously short distance but whether I would actually finish at all. If the answer was yes, was I going to be able to put my head back in the water and switch back to freestyle or would I actually continue to clown around in breaststroke, despite three swim practices a week?

While wrestling through that 1500-meter course, a thought clearly formulated in my head that I would not do an Ironman! "Heck, I would even turn back right here as the shore would still be closer as opposed to swimming the whole course. But I just can't do that – what would I tell my "family support team"? I'm not a person who gives up, I have no choice, I have to go through with it. I have already signed up for the race in Nagyatád. How am I going to tell everyone that I have changed my mind?" While these thoughts were circling in my head, 32 minutes had passed, and I somehow managed to pull myself ashore.

I waved, pretending that I was having fun, and I was off for the bike ride. I heard that it was a difficult 40-km course (25 miles), which was challenging with respect to both bike handling and climbing abilities. However exciting that may sound, none of that increased my "appetite," and no matter how short the bike course was, I assumed it was going to suck. I was right! My watch logged a near 1700 feet elevation gain over the course, but I was able to do that at around a 19-mph average speed, which was pushing my boundaries. My average heart rate ended up in the highest zone and it was clear that I pushed myself during the biking phase way beyond the reasonable. During the race, I got stung by a wasp, I saw multiple riders crash trying to negotiate the difficult course, and I played "can you pass me" with one of my teammates, who seldom came to practice and who I later learned was more a cyclist than a triathlete! Perhaps this was one of the reasons why I pushed myself to the edge, which came back to bite me in the butt during the run.

I did not have great aspirations about the race to start with, neither was I highly motivated. Since all that was left was the 10K run, I took

Hibernated Life and Derailed Dress Rehearsals

it for granted that I would eat it up at a sub 8:00 minutes per mile pace. Executing that pace was quite a different story – nonetheless, I managed to pull it off. The truth is, it wasn't even the run that I was thinking about, but rather how I should carry on after the event was over! "Where did this swim come from?! I go to the pool three times a week and each time I swim more than that! What more can I do? This kind of start to a race takes everything out of me so if that happens in Nagyatád, all the preparations and the invested time and energy would go down the drain. Somehow, I must overcome this subconscious panicking! Somehow..."

I didn't care about my finishing time, which was 2 hours 50 minutes. After I sent off the training week data, the reply from Ákos was simply: "It looks like your biking is coming along nicely, but you should have put a bit more effort into the run..."

To put it mildly, there was nothing that could stimulate me anymore. I only cared about the race in Nagyatád. As a crowning of my repeat "success" at Velence, just as I was on my way to the transition area to get out my bike, I heard my name and bib number announced from the stage over the PA system. I won a slot for the 2017 Velence race. I went up, expressed my gratitude, but didn't know whether I should laugh or cry.

A WEEKEND PROGRAM? I'M ALL SET, THANK YOU

My training weeks looked fairly identical. On Mondays, I was resting pretty much the whole day. I had only one gym session in the evening. Tuesdays, I just wanted over with because that was the day when I had to both ride and run after swimming (which made for half-a-day of nearly continuous training). On Wednesdays, I only had a few hours of biking. I actually looked forward to the Thursday swim and evening team run. After the Friday morning swim, I was able to rest. The latter was much needed, too, because with the nearing of the Ironman, my weekends became brutal. The Saturday after my triumphant Velence race, for instance, I had to ride around

Confessions of an Ironman

90 miles and then go out for a half-hour run, doing it all in specific heart rate zones.

These Saturday sessions filled up a good part of 6 hours, and the weather didn't make the preparations easy. There was nothing that could make me go riding in the rain, so when the weather called for it, I set up the home trainer, loaded the merciless Hawaii course, and rode those 90 miles in the middle of my living room. This "home court" advantage enabled me to freely test all kinds of different nutrition plans, as I did not have to worry about getting sick somewhere far away, like in neighboring Slovakia where we once rode.

To be completely honest, it took a lot to convince myself to spend 5-6 hours inside, on that machine, when all my teammates said it would be insane to go biking in such weather or similarly to get on a trainer for that long. For me, it was never an option *not* to complete what the training plan dictated. The Hawaii bike course proved to be an interesting ride because the biking was either about frantic downhill speeding or backbreaking climbs. The 90 miles included nearly 4000 feet of elevation and when I got off the bike with a 17 mph average speed flashing on the display, my knees and ankles were not in the best shape – for sure, not in an ideal condition for the run that was to follow.

Will Power Can Only Get You So Far! You Need Something More

Many believe that sheer will power can help them achieve great things, but I have read in many places that this source is finite, it does not last forever. Some around me say that what I've achieved is the triumph of will, but I think they are mistaken. In my case, there was always something greater in the background of all my goals, and will power alone would not have been enough to carry me through.

Hibernated Life and Derailed Dress Rehearsals

This "greater" thing was such a profoundly strong motivation, such an inviting and powerful vision that never stopped pulling me. While will power can run out as time passes, this "pull of motivation" is an inexhaustible resource. What's also true is that I could not have found that kind of motivation for simply any goal, but for those aspirations of mine which are rooted in that source, the outcome is indisputable.

What I felt in the gravity of the Ironman was that it would finally enable me to see myself as a person who is good enough; it would help me put down a load I had been carrying and move on with my life, finally satisfied. Will power had nothing to do with that! I recommend you always strive to uncover your deepest motivations that are behind your goals. Those motivations will give you the power to keep going through the most difficult of times.

On Sunday, I ran 19 miles and completed a roughly 20-hour training week. I messaged Ákos that my ankles and knees seemed to be on their last rope, and that I was a little concerned about them – I also added that I was beyond exhausted. I let him know that I had an invitation to a wedding for the following Saturday, so I could not fit anything similar into the following weekend's program, even if I wanted to.

Ask Questions, Learn, and Use What Has Proven to Work!

Muscle soreness became completely natural during my long months of preparation. Mostly, my thighs ached and I was not entirely alone with that problem. My more experienced teammates had a number of solutions for these sorts of

Confessions of an Ironman

problems; all I had to do was ask for their advice. For some reason, I waited too long (once again).

Eventually, I learned two things that seemed to work well. One was the so-called SMR roller,[11] the use of which proved to be just as torturous a process as the long training sessions preceding, and which I used to help my muscles recover faster and be somewhat ready for the next adversity. It is easy to find a heap of information about the benefits of the use of this device, and what kinds of exercises can be done with it. It is a large, cylinder-shaped roller which, using one's own body weight, can inflict all kinds of pain ... and achieve deep-tissue massage effects. (When I got my hands on my own red and black specimen, complete with ridges and knobs, the cleaning lady who turns up at my house every once in a while exclaimed, "How pretty!" She thought it was a floor vase.)

The second solution was one that Robi shared in the last phase of my preparation. He knew a place where they specialized in sports massage for an affordable price. That also proved to be very painful. The day after each session, my muscles felt sorer than before. But the next day, I felt renewed and so it was worth every cent. The secret was not to schedule a massage for the day before any hard training. I ended up being a regular customer for a few months and I especially enjoyed the extreme stories told by the girls.

The wedding "saved" me from the "double shift" the following weekend, even if some of the assignments got moved to the preceding weekdays. On Saturday, while the female members of the wedding guests were busy getting ready, I did an 80-minute run at gradually increasing tempo to kill some time, making my way from the village where we were to the Austrian border and back.

---

[11] The abbreviation stands for *Self-Myofascial Release*.

Hibernated Life and Derailed Dress Rehearsals

By this time, I also learned – during the Balaton loop, actually – that I had more endurance than my Garmin Forerunner 920 sports watch. It was obvious that it would not last through the whole Ironman adventure on a single charge; I had to think of something. Adjusting my finishing time to accommodate the battery life was clearly out of the question (I would be the world champion if that was possible), therefore I picked the easier route. It was around that time Anikó started to believe that she, too, was a triathlete, and had decided to change her simple sports watch to something that had more functions. Luckily, she had not gone completely mad and did not want to do any long-distance events, therefore my watch was perfect for her, which meant that I could get my hands on the Fenix 3, which I immediately fell in love with. This purchase was just as needless and irrational as my buying the Forerunner when I could not even swim one length in a 36-yard pool without stopping, but these gadgets also served as wonderful little motivational tools! Wearing a watch like this for the first time, it was not an option not to swim my very first 1500-meter freestyle in the pool. That investment alone had already solidified my commitment to the project, but I went and raised the bar even further, yet again.

Dress for Success!

I heard, over the course of numerous seminars, how strong the effects of external things are on our way of thinking and how they can be turned to our own advantage. Here is an extreme example: You feel utterly different wearing a luxury suit as opposed to a worn-out warm-up set and, consequently, you behave differently, too.

Many "success gurus" recommend that those who are in pursuit of wealth and prosperity buy one or two premium quality outfits, which they can still afford, instead of spending that same sum of money on heaps of low-end clothing. The feeling of making

Confessions of an Ironman

---

the purchase will be entirely different, just like the feeling when "gearing up." It is worth trying, I think, as it can spark some very interesting recognitions.

The notion of "dress for success" caught up with me in a rather "underdressed" phase of my life, during the Ironman preparation. When I undertook my first 1500 meters at the BVSC pool, all I wore were my swimming trunks and my Garmin Forerunner 920. Wearing that watch had already made me an Ironman; it was not an option to get out of the pool before I was done.

It was during that week – lightened up because of the wedding – when I first got a chance to try the Fenix 3. Initially, I loved everything about it. Later, on Wednesday, after my 3-hour bike ride, just before I hit the road for the prescribed off-the-bike run, I glanced at it to see the session summary and saw that my new friend measured a near 13,000-feet elevation gain for the 51.5-mile ride. It was interesting, because I rode the usual route, which had not been reshaped by the addition of any hills or mountains. Surely I would have noticed 13,000 feet of climbing, if for no other reason than simply because I would have dropped dead halfway through.

I called the guys at Garmin to see what could be done. They told me they had never heard of the barometric altimeter malfunctioning on the watch, although the problem I described clearly pointed that way. I went to see them, and while we had a good talk riding an elevator up and down a few times, we found that the altimeter was indeed out of whack. After a swift exchange for a new watch, accompanied by perfect customer service, I loved using the Fenix 3.

"YOU DO A HALF IRONMAN JUST FOR TRAINING?"

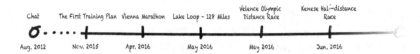

Most people I knew had basically given up any hope of seeing me; they probably knew we would only be able to spend "undisturbed" time together after the Ironman. Still, every now and again, they did make an attempt. During the last, light week of the eighth training cycle some friends were going to Lake Balaton for the weekend and asked if we would like to join them.

They were very happy when I told them that we'd be at Lake Balaton that weekend as well, in a town called Kenese. Disappointment soon followed as I also told them I'd be doing a Half Ironman there because it was my Saturday training plan.

Ákos really eased off that week because I'm sure he thought that, after resting up for the race, I would surely drive myself into the ground on Saturday anyways. As far as the resting part of the plan was concerned, I executed it perfectly, but I didn't have any specific expectations for the race. I thought of it as any other training day, and basically saw it as an ideal test opportunity in many respects.

This quick summary of my Kenese project is proof that I am not the sort of athlete ready to burst at the seams from an overload of competitive attitude, looking for opportunities to supersede his opponents. Here is what I wished to accomplish: Finish before the Hungary-Iceland European Championship soccer match started – after all, it was not very often that our national team qualified for such events; get through the swim in an agreeable mental state (I didn't care about the speed, but I did need a positive aquatic experience before Nagyatád); and test the bottled up, gel-mixture nutrition plan, also known as the "Ironman Secret" during the bike leg.

Confessions of an Ironman

I had to have been a "dream client" to a coach with a genuine competitor's mentality. Wetsuits were needed for the swim and the extremely simple strategy, formulated with Peti, a teammate who was also getting ready for Nagyatád, included starting from far to the side to avoid the serious "meat grinder" and swim the 1900 meters in relatively smooth conditions over the two-lap course. On a swim course like that, the start and maybe the first lap can make a difference. By the second lap, the field gets adequately dispersed due to the differences in swimming abilities, and it was less likely that we'd get kicked around. After my repeated panicky experience in Velence, I was especially afraid of this part of the race, but this time I managed to pull it off fairly well. I completed the first discipline without any major complications, and Peti and I got out of the water together after 42 minutes. We usually swam at the same tempo during practice, too.

As for the bike, all I wanted was to be reassured that, compared to my previous – and so far only – half-distance race, the Budapest 70.3, I became stronger. I did not expect the 56 miles to take much out of me. I felt I should be able to easily do the run afterwards, especially with the new gel magic on board. The bike course consisted of three loops, but it was far from flat and there was a lot of wind. Just to make sure I had not forgotten, the ride reminded me that I still did not like biking. I had a lot of time on my hands to think about that, so I came to an amusing decision: "As soon as I cross the finish line in Nagyatád, I will sell the bike, right there."

The benefits of the gel mixture were clear: It worked well. I followed the "instructions" and I also drank a lot of water with it, so it turned out – for the first time in my life – that my refueling was without blemishes. Nonetheless, halfway through the bike, I still felt I'd rather swap the whole thing for a really long run, even though everyone else always said that it was the run that required the most energy. But that, at least, I enjoyed.

My bike time was a tad fast for me, 2 hours 50 minutes, which meant that I probably pushed it a bit harder than I should have.

Hibernated Life and Derailed Dress Rehearsals

Despite the pace, I did not feel fatigued when I was getting ready for the run. It was entertaining to hear some of the expert advice that friends and relatives shouted here and there from a grassy area outside the transition area. My favorite one came from the girlfriend of this guy who was right beside me in the transition area – the volume level of her *"hydrate for the love of God"* was commendable. Having to listen to this repeatedly, we came to the conclusion that he'd better pour something in or, if nothing else, on himself quickly so that she would stop.

As usual, I started the run faster than I should have, but knowing from experience where that could lead, I slowed down just as quickly. As strange as it may seem, that was when my problems started: Looking at my watch, I realized I was "way ahead of schedule" for the soccer game, and there was nothing I could do to miss it. It was also evident that I could only beat my previous half-distance time – on that much more demanding course – if I went all out. Since that was out of the question, the whole half-marathon act lost its meaning, there was nothing to make me push myself. I started giving high-fives to kids standing around, I spotted a girl from my hometown and said hello, I ate and drank everything I could at the aid stations, so, in the end, I could hardly move. It took me 1 hour and 52 minutes to complete the half-marathon run, and I clocked 5 hours and 31 minutes total in the end. Although I did not die from the race, I must admit that being able to cover double that distance in a respectable amount of time in a few weeks still felt unimaginable to me.

I made quick arrangements with the officials who were guarding the equipment in the transition area that I would get my bike out only when the soccer match was over – after all, I couldn't sit down for a beer with all my gear, my bike, and a soaked wetsuit. They smiled and thought I was nuts, although I was not the only one with similar thoughts. Some of the slower finishers had actually taken detours from the running course to nearby bars and pubs just to be able to glance at the TV screens to see how our team was doing.

Confessions of an Ironman

After sending my Garmin data, Ákos' reply came back saying that I was on the right track, since my biking was still projected to improve. He also expressed hope that I would finally put in a decent run. I was yet to learn how one could put in a "decent" run as the last discipline of a triathlon, but I didn't let that bother me since it was the panic attack on the swim, and the length of the bike ride that worried me more. As for the run, I was certain that if only a marathon stood between me and the completion of an Ironman, I would definitely be able to do it.

I Saw, I Came (Back), I Won!

After Kenese, Ákos said something along the lines of secretly hoping for an 11-hour Ironman time. This mental anchor did not grab me anymore – not one bit. The time left until the race was so short that this "new goal" seemed insurmountable.

Psychology and the mind are huge factors on the road to success, that is certain. It is quite different if one is in it for the win or is just there, playing it safe. I have already shared my self-image issues with you, which were rooted in my childhood clumsiness, and I was clearly a member of the latter group. My Kenese race had also proven that I would never get into serious competitions with others. (I play the safe game in the world of investing, too: I don't gamble with my money in hopes of extraordinary profits. Instead, I go for the predictable and stable dividend income. I get outstanding results this way, not to mention that it all happens without constant worrying or the investment activity taking up all of my time.)

Do you still remember the eye-opening game I played at the promotional session of Tony Robbins' London event? Playing that game, in the beginning of 2014, I clearly saw that I could not win with the strategy I chose, so I gave in and just wanted the game to end. In the meantime, the truths that the game revealed bothered me beyond belief as they were shocking, so I definitely wanted to learn from that experience. Within one year, in the beginning of November, they put on the same satellite event. By then, I had gone through my learning in London as well as countless other adventures, so my main reason in participating was to find out if I could learn anything new. There was no way to know in advance that they'd pull out that same game again, with the same rules, just as before. When it was announced, my stomach bunched up in a knot; I did not want to relive my previous experience! While I knew exactly why I lost last time, and I had a fairly good idea how winning might be possible, I still couldn't be sure that my approach would result in success. I very seriously considered not taking part in the game because the pain it inflicted before was still vivid in my memory. In the end, I did not back down, played courageously, and ended up winning in a crowd of over a hundred. I went up to the stage, openly admitted that I had played before, and told everyone what I had learned and what my applied winning strategy was. Finally, I accepted the valuable prize, which I gave away before the end of the event.

I learned my lesson from the previous shock: I did not crumble, I did not cop out and flee; instead, I stood up, dusted myself off, and won! That is my strength. While others soak in long-lasting self-pity as they lick their wounds after a few small slaps in the face, I quickly get over things I cannot alter, and instead of feeling sorry for myself, I try to focus on what the situation can teach me. It was no different when I was still in the horrendously expensive phase of finding the right path to my financial goals. It had happened that the price of a nice big car disappeared from my investment account in only a few hours' time, but the next day I was still able to open a new document on my computer to take notes on what I had learned and what

Confessions of an Ironman

> I would do differently from that point on. The pain was there, unmistakably. But I had to move on, I had to learn because otherwise my sacrifice would have been in vain. This approach has always worked for me, in every aspect of my life.

Naturally, I was curious whether I would get fired up and want to "race" in Nagyatád, or simply settle for going the distance. For the time being, I was trying to focus on what came next: I had five training weeks left, and the race fell on the sixth one. Ákos took this chunk of time and divided it up into two 2+1-week training cycles, which meant that the Ironman fell on the Saturday of the final, lightened-up week of my tenth training cycle.

LET'S SEE THE COURSE!

I was very interested in two specific parts of the race course. One was the bike route, which I had heard quite a bit about, and the other was the water, where around 700 athletes would get started on their big adventure all at the same time. I had a hunch that my sense of comfort would greatly improve if I got a feel for both, so I decided that on the first week of the ninth training cycle I would do my Saturday long ride on location. We booked a room in Gyékényes, a small village near the border, where the race starts each year with the swim in an artificial but beautiful lake. From there, the course takes the competitors to Nagyatád (about 47 miles away) where three smaller loops await them to complete the 112-mile bike ride.

Basically, everyone I talked to was in agreement that the first section of the bike course was the trickiest, but their reasons why varied quite a bit. Some thought that the road quality was the most troublesome, while others were convinced that the elevation made it difficult. It was a most fortunate coincidence that Ákos had prescribed a 95-mile bike session for Saturday, so I made plans to do an out-and-back between Gyékényes and Nagyatád.

The owner of the place where we stayed seemed very accommodating over the phone, but when we got our keys Friday evening, she kept telling us to make sure we were out by noon the next day. We knew the room was not booked after us, still, the lady felt that it would only be fair if she charged an overly large percentage of the daily room price for every additional hour we

Confessions of an Ironman

spent there. She pulled this stunt despite the fact that I had told her in advance I would not be back by noon on Saturday, plus we had decided that Anikó would take care of breakfast for me when I got back, and we'd only leave after eating and a quick shower. Paying what the lady asked was simply out of the question, since we had previously agreed otherwise on the phone.

I woke up very early the next day, so the sun was just beginning to dawn when I was already fixing my magic gel cocktail. I reviewed the route on Google Maps for the umpteenth time, then hit the road a few minutes after 6:00 a.m. I was alone, which was not unusual, but being in a completely new place was uncomfortable. Despite my thorough pre-work as to what settlements I was to go through, I still stopped from time to time to make sure I was in the right place. The first part of the course included a forested section, which was a beautiful nature preserve, so it was very exciting to be the first human to appear there in the morning, causing a peaceful little commotion among the animals. The screams, shouts, and squeaks were so unnerving, though, that I didn't really have to think twice whether or not to stop – my motivation to push on hard was rock solid.

The weather was still all right when I got to Nagyatád, where I made a stop at a gas station to replenish my water supplies before I turned around. There was a motorbike gang making a stop there who, seeming quite genuine, were humbled by my efforts and told me that they would feel very disheartened if they'd have to get on that *thing* with those hair-thin wheels to have to pedal all the way back to Gyékényes from there.

The course was quite manageable. There was a noticeable hill in the beginning and the road quality wasn't spotless, but all in all, I felt there wasn't much to worry about. The ride was 5 hours and 16 minutes, which stretched to 5 hours 25 minutes with the addition of the gas station stop. When I got back, I would have had about 15 minutes to eat my breakfast and shower if we were to take the host's warning seriously, but, by that time, I was relaxed enough to

Let's See the Course!

simply tell her that although her efforts to make us pay more were valiant, we still had to regretfully decline, as our agreement finalized before our arrival was not in line with them. We comfortably packed up our things, gave our key back, and went down to the lake.

I definitely wanted to test the water. Everyone, without exception, had said that it was comfortably warm and crystal clear, so the swim part of the race could not appear more ideal. Except for the crowd of 700, of course. My plan was to have a light swim after the tough bike ride and then we could be on our way home. Anikó and I decided that we would swim out to a small island, but she fell behind or went back, so I was on my own when I got there. I turned around, picked out a landmark on the shore, and began to swim. After a while it became very suspicious that even though I had been swimming for much longer than on the way there, the shore still appeared to be quite far. Not to mention that as I got closer and closer, the emerging coastline looked much different than when I originally entered the water. I was lost in the lake, and this time my GPS watch didn't prove to be of any help.

I couldn't think what to do, so I swam to shore, where a half-naked, elderly man was fishing from the backyard of his property. He had quite a few hooks in the water, which made it somewhat difficult to negotiate my disembarkation. It was clear that he began to panic while watching me try to avoid his fishing lines as I swam closer and closer. By the time I found solid ground, the whole family was lined up to greet me as I emerged from the water, in my trunks, and posing my embarrassing question: "Where am I?" If I had had my phone, I would have certainly taken a picture of those dumbfounded faces. Since I did not, I thought I'd quickly ask for one and call Anikó to tell her not to worry, because sooner or later I would get there, although I had no idea where I was or which direction I should be headed.

After some hesitation, they did get me a phone, which only helped me prove the scientific hypothesis, in the presence of a greater audience, that women do not answer their calls when most needed.

Confessions of an Ironman

I gave it a few tries, but later learned that Anikó was basking in the sun with her phone in silent mode right next to her. I had to turn back to my new "hosts" with inquiries as to which way I should continue.

They suggested that I walk along the shore; that way, I would eventually find the spot where I got into the water. Being barefoot, with the midday sun mercilessly beating down and the pavement burning hot, I decided to pass on that idea. Instead, I asked them to show me the direction I should aim for if I was to continue back in the water. My task turned out to be fairly simple, as there was only one place, according to them, where I could have gotten in the water. All I had to do was swim about 1100 yards to reach that spot. As the wife launched into an almost-convincing lament about how I shouldn't attempt that because I was surely way too exhausted to make it back without drowning, and how it would be a disaster to have to search for my floating corpse in their beautiful lake, I thought I'd leave it to the husband to calm her down. Just to pour some more oil on the fire, before I dove back into the water, I turned around and said, "I have already ridden about 6 hours this morning, too." As a result, instead of a nice cooldown in the water, I ended up with a 2800 yard swim, which took the better part of an hour. When I got out, I asked Anikó not to call the number from which she had received a few rings. After telling her about my unplanned adventure, we had lunch and hit the road home. It was only when we were already home that I learned, looking at the map in my Garmin app, that my getting lost got me on the (two-lap) swim course of the Ironman, which not only did I complete, but made it even farther with my less-than-straight swim in the lake.

After thinking it over, I concluded the water was pleasant and just as clear as I had been told. I could see everything (even the fishing lines); the bike course also seemed manageable. I closed out my week with a 15.5-mile light run, which felt very good and gave me an opportunity to mull over all that had happened. I was ready for the next week.

WE OUTGREW THE COUNTRY

During that phase of training, I was mainly interested in what the weekend program had to offer, and it never failed to cause "excitement." Before the lighter week of the second-to-last cycle, I still had to ride 105 miles on Saturday, followed by a 19-mile run on Sunday. I was really hoping the weather would allow for a ride outside; doing 105 miles on the trainer would have been brutal, not to mention boring. Nevertheless, the daunting question of where I could actually bike 105 miles still lingered. I had never gone more than roughly 70 miles on my standard route, and I didn't really miss that hilly terrain. It was exciting to hear Peti's idea to roll out to neighboring Slovakia on a road that he already knew.

It was an amusing adventure. We met up around 7:00 a.m. at a spot in the city near the Danube River. We reviewed the route quickly because we wanted to make it as far into the ride as possible before the sun got burning hot. It was obvious Peti would take the lead, as he was the one who knew which way to go. We went through Szentendre and Visegrád; as we were making our way toward Esztergom, some very interesting thoughts circled in my head. While still riding in Budapest, it would have been enough to name the street if anyone asked where I was coming from. Nearing the Danube bend up north, I would have certainly had to add the city, too. Crossing the border into Slovakia, the country would have also

Confessions of an Ironman

had to be identified. Not even in my wildest dreams would I have ever thought that one day I'd ride my bike across the border into a different country, and still get back home around noon.

Along less-complicated sections of the route, where the road was as straight as an arrow for long miles, we kept switching turns at the front. It wasn't a good idea, because I don't really know how to take it easy on the bike, especially over such long distances, as it makes me think I have to go hard if I ever want the ride to be over. We were still on the Hungarian side when we stopped at a gas station to buy some isotonic drinks. We quickly agreed that the pace I dictated was beginning to hurt us both, and since the route was about to get a bit trickier from there, I should only take the front on the way home. In Slovakia, besides the fact that the drivers are more careful when around cyclists, the quality of the roads was also much better. During that section of the ride, we pretty much focused only on our odometers to see when they turned to 53 miles; that marked the halfway point where we could immediately turn around. We did just that, but our struggles really began on the way home as it had gotten very hot by then. We kept looking for fountains and consumed very large amounts of water. We were on the bikes for 5 hours and 47 minutes, and as we arrived back at our meeting point, we both admitted that neither of us felt like we would be up for a marathon at that point – or anything else for that matter – which was less than reassuring three weeks out from the race. In my training plan, the time allotted for this little Saturday ride was seven hours. Clearly, we had gotten carried away a little, and we should have taken it much easier.

I decided to do my Sunday 19-miler run on Margaret Island, the place with the horrid memories of my "suicidal" marathon preparation. I went there because, similarly to the Nagyatád running course, I could do near 5K laps, which made it easier to gauge how I felt after each lap over that long distance. I could easily get a session like that out of the way in the morning and have the rest of the day off.

We Outgrew the Country

"He Just Doesn't Stop Eating! I Can't Wait Until He Runs Out."

The statement was made by an older man – most likely a fanatic Trekky – sitting two seats away from me during the showing of the newest *Star Trek* movie. I was trying to recover from one of my long weekend programs and eating everything in sight.

I ate a lot during the last part of the Ironman preparation. Sometimes I had to hold myself back so that I wouldn't eat ten servings in only two sittings because that just seemed way overboard. One time, Anikó called and asked me to go out to dinner to celebrate something after I had already had my dinner; it didn't even cross my mind to say no. I ordered my three courses, as usual, ate them all, plus whatever Anikó hadn't finished. My weight never changed, though, which is probably due to my build, but also because I burned an incredible number of calories.

My more spiritual-minded friends said my overeating was compensation for my self-punishing Ironman adventure, but I simply thought my body was in constant fear of getting exposed to a 5-6 hour bike ride, and loaded up with calories when it got any opportunity to take something on board. Around that time, I read a book about the psychology of eating and the related irrational behaviors. It talked about some very frightening experiments and conclusions – I actually think it should be a compulsory reading for those with weight and/or eating problems.[12] It was quite entertaining, too, so I went ahead and tried out a few practices it listed and they seemed to work very well. In the end, I gave in to the same conclusion noted in the book, namely that it is mainly those who do not exercise who tend to apply various mind tricks to control consumed calories. I am fine, as I work out plenty. Nonetheless, the book also insinuates it might be easier to convince its target audience to

---

[12] Brian Wansink, *Mindless Eating: Why We Eat More Than We Think.*

Confessions of an Ironman

> apply a few functional tricks than to persuade them to get off of the couch.
>
> My food consumption returned to normal a few weeks (or months?) after the Ironman.

It did not surprise me much that the "light" week prior to my last cycle included 12 hours of training. In contrast to the preceding nearly 20-hour training weeks, this was a clearly detectable lightening in the workload, and the intensity of the sessions was not the same. I was in agreement with Ákos that it would most likely boost my self-confidence if I included a full 112-mile bike ride in my training. I cannot say it was unexpected that the first weekend of the tenth, and final, cycle included the "dream program": 112 miles of biking on Saturday, and 25 miles of running on Sunday. This made for an over 20-hour training week with a few added twists: We had an invitation to a 60th birthday party on Saturday afternoon, which had to be jammed in between the 112-mile ride and the 25-mile run, on the other side of the country. It was a weekend on all counts, and as such all I could tell Anikó was that I had no idea when I would get done riding, so she better take me out of the equation for the weekend. We were in for some charming conversations for Monday, Tuesday, Wednesday, Thursday, and Friday, until I woke up on Saturday to realize that it was pouring outside.

Peti and I exchanged a few text messages and decided that we would cancel the "team" ride, and he would go right back to bed. I, on the other hand, did not have that option. It was beyond any question whether I would get out in the rain, not to mention that I did not have any 112-mile routes in my bag. The only thing left was my emergency solution of a tire switch on my bike; thereafter the home trainer was set up, the Hawaii course loaded, nutrition stacked up in the middle of my living room, and while Anikó was still sleeping, let the biking begin. The later she got up, the better

We Outgrew the Country

because at least she wouldn't be besieging me with "When will you be done? When do you think we can leave for the party?" questions, which I could not answer. That was the only time I actually completed the whole course that I got as a "gift" with the virtual trainer. It took 6 hours and 51 minutes to cover the full distance with its 4691 feet of elevation gain. I had a whole lot of time on my hands to think through if there was a living soul on this planet who thought that this Hawaii course DVD could actually be a gift. If so, I'd make them ride it every single day.

As for the birthday party, everything went well. I was recovering for the Sunday 25-mile run, wearing compression socks, and could have gotten a restroom assigned to my name due to the unpleasant side effects of the barbarous amounts of gels that I had consumed. (If you have not had the pleasure to experience anything like this, for a few bucks, you can easily give it a try. It was only a couple of weeks before the Ironman when I had learned there was a manufacturer that only used natural ingredients in their products, so they do not cause any bloating, and – as the shop assistant put it – "you can even go among people after using them." Nonetheless, I did not want to take any risks right before the race, so I kept using what had proven to work for me.)

I KNEW IT WAS WELL WITHIN MY REACH, AND I IMMEDIATELY WANTED MORE!

To be honest, after going through this 112 plus 25-mile weekend, I started feeling that I was actually capable of completing an Ironman race. Assuming there were no technical difficulties on the bike, I felt physically prepared to do it. As soon as the thought entered my mind that my original goal was within reach, I began to ponder what finishing time I could feasibly shoot for.

I had all kinds of numbers in my head. The basic math was that I would surely finish the 2.4-mile swim somewhere around 1.5 hours, I would go for a 6-hour time over the 112-mile bike ride (or finish it perhaps with a few minutes over that), and my marathon time would be in the ballpark of 4 hours. This would make for 11.5 hours plus the time in the two transitions. I calculated that if all went well, I could stay inside 12 hours; the 11.5-hour time that Ákos envisioned at the beginning of the project did not feel realistic.[13]

I constructed a three-level goal system in my head, but my true realization of what that really meant only came while tossing and

---

[13] To put things in perspective, here are some times a professional triathlete is capable of: In the 2015 Nagyatád race, Márton Flander, the winner that year, started with a 50-minute swim, then he clocked a 4-hour 35-minute bike ride, and ran a marathon just under 3 hours, which resulted in an 8-hour 29-miute overall finishing time.

I Knew It Was Well Within My Reach

turning the night before the race. My primary goal was to finish the race; that would already be deserving of a big tick next to the "Ironman entry" on my bucket list. My secondary goal, since I had put so much work into this, was that I certainly did not want to stretch the race beyond 13 hours! The ultimate goal was that I would somehow manage to get under the 12-hour mark at the finish line. I ended up contemplating the latter goal a bit more than I should have; being a complete amateur, my time didn't matter much at all. Nonetheless, I tinkered with the time question just to prove something to myself and perhaps because I did not want to finish slower than my teammates who were at the same level as I.

There was another lighter home trainer weekend when we "borrowed" my little brother Bence, who adorably kept asking during my 2.5-3 hour roller session what he could hand me to eat or drink. Following some handy work in the kitchen, he hurried to my aid with such enthusiasm that he dropped the sandwiches he made right on the wooden floor face down, and he threw the dissolving tablets into the drinks he was mixing with such energy that nearly the whole apartment got flooded. In the midst of these funny scenes he also asked me how long I figured this Ironman race was going to take. That was when I first articulated that it would be about 12 hours; from that moment on, in Bence's brain, it was simply regarded as the "12-hour race." The 12-hour quote had burned into my brain, and I really did not want to have to ultimately explain why my "12-hour-race" took 13 hours instead.

During the final phase of preparations, Ákos mentioned that, in his opinion, an 11-hour time wasn't too far-fetched, either. His opinion did not make much of a difference at that point because it was far beyond the level that I could take seriously.

I did my best to gather as much information, experience, and advice as possible from my teammates. Most of them had already completed so many Ironman races that, despite their most genuine efforts, they couldn't quite put themselves in my shoes. This was one of the reasons why it was so fortunate that Robi, whose name

Confessions of an Ironman

came up in connection with those brutal bike rides mentioned earlier, had decided to undertake the Ironman Austria, held weeks before the Nagyatád race. He would be able to tell me all about the experiences he gained as a "first-timer." My most valuable learning was that with the amount of training I had completed, it was without question that my body would be able to get me through the race. Robi had also seen people who were much less prepared yet still able to complete the long course. This was very reassuring to hear, just like when he told me that the colossal quantity of gel solution worked perfectly during the bike ride. Robi also got a flat, which was not very fortunate as it took him a long time to fix his tire in the rainy weather. He recommended that we take some CO_2 canisters with us because using those could save quite a bit of time in case we found ourselves in a similar situation. (At that point, there was nothing I would not have purchased that could possibly prove to be helpful.) My problem was that no matter how hard I tried, I could not figure out how I could carry a bottle filled with the gel solution, another one with clear water, plus one more filled with my isotonic drink, all at the same time. I only had two bottle holders on my bike.

On Dangerous Waters

After the 2015 Budapest half-distance race, many of my teammates had remarked that my bike time was not too bad, considering I was a rookie and rode without aerobars. Apparently, when using this device, considerable time could be saved over a 56-mile bike ride, which obviously made it a must over the full-distance race.

My only problem with aerobars was that I had no idea what type I should get; I had also been warned that it took some getting used to before I would be able to keep my bike on a straight line when using them. In hindsight, I consider it a miracle that I managed to survive the learning phase without any serious accidents. I was crazy enough to begin my testing in the most impossible situations: For instance, going downhill, doing over 30 mph, where my adrenaline levels were skyrocketing and I could not keep my bike from waddling frantically all over the place.

Months passed before I even touched the aerobars on the bike during my rides. Finally, when the time pressure became unmistakable, from session to session, I made myself spend more and more time in the aero position, so I started to make progress there, too. By the time the Kenese race arrived, I was beginning to feel somewhat more comfortable with them. By the end of my Ironman training, I was quite at ease putting my elbows down on those pads.

As a contrast, it only took me about a half hour to get used to the double bottle holder placed behind the saddle (the installation of which solved the "three bottles two holders" puzzle), and, fortunately, the CO_2 canister pumps I never had to use.

BEFORE THE RACE, OVER THE PEAK

Following the pinnacle week, the workloads subsided for the final "proper" training week. We went out on Saturday for a light 60-miler ride, and on Sunday I ran 11 miles on my usual creek route. In my mind I was in Nagyatád already; I could not even talk about anything else. My friends pointed out that it seemed as though I was a bit afraid of the whole thing.

When race week arrived, I was willing to do the Thursday swim, but after that we were on our way to Csokonyavisonta, a small village a little ways from Nagyatád where we had booked our lodging. I was very happy to learn that the race organizers had arranged a viewing of the running course for that same day, because I really wanted to see the course before the race. That easy, early evening jog put the

Confessions of an Ironman

final piece of the puzzle in place. The picture of the whole course was now in my head, and all that was left for me to do was to follow it from start to end on Saturday. Time seemed to slow down, and thoughts about what and how I should do were perpetually circling in my head. Before the Friday half-hour easy spin, for example, I worried that my triathlon racing singlet was very nice and all but it gave me really bad chafing during the half-distance race. By the time I got to the run, it made every step painful as the saddle padding rubbed against the base of my thigh. I decided that I'd wear my almost thigh-long swim trunks under the singlet, hoping that the additional layer would solve the problem – never mind that a mere half-hour bike ride could never reveal if this sort of thing would actually work. Nonetheless, I made up my mind – I would wear them to launch into the adventure the next day.

There was one more event left until the last evening before the Ironman: Gábor Kindl's presentation on race nutrition for endurance sports. I definitely did not want to miss that, although looking back now, I would have been better off if I had. He said very useful things, but at that point I had already had a tested, well-working system: 6 packs of gels in a bottle, diluted in water, which I take a drink of every half-hour on the bike and wash it down with plenty of water. My experience showed that there weren't any problems with that combination. However, what I gathered from Kindl's presentation was that if the solution is not mixed in the proper ratio, as he said, "you will put deadly poison in your body," which would not be processed. Instead, it would be rejected either through the front or the back side, much sooner than expected, and would drain my power tank rather than serve as a source of energy. No matter how hard I tried, I could not make the math work when I put the portions of my recipe into the formula shown in the presentation (including the added wash-down water). The words "deadly poison" had burned themselves into my brain, and on the way back to our lodging, I was in deep contemplation: "Should I risk changing my trusted gel recipe?" The presentation was professional and seemed scientifically irrefutable, which did not put me at ease. Being well aware of the manifesting power of words, I was not very happy that the expression "deadly poison" had nested in my mind, similar to my worries at the Jászberény marathon when the "heatwave warning" was explicitly announced.

I did not have much time to make a decision as I had made plans to prepare the magic mix that evening, knowing how busy I would be the next morning. I could not think of a better solution than going half-way between the two – I put less gel in the bottle and decided to drink even more water so as to make sure that the cocktail was further thinned down. I cannot say I was totally comfortable with this mixture, since it was surely less potent and I could not be certain that it would have the same refueling results.

To Persist or to Be Open to New Ways?

It is worth devoting time to see how we can find balance between sticking to our proven solutions and being open to learning from experts. This question frequently emerges in many areas of our lives.

Generally, I experiment with newfound information, but the "race of my life" was clearly not the ideal place for that. I had similar reasons not to change to natural ingredient-based gels in the final stretch of my preparation; there was not enough time to test if they would provide me with enough energy, and to see how my stomach would react to them during such a long race. I would have needed at least a marathon or a half-distance race to put them to the test.

My plan was to go to bed early and the alarm was set to 4:00 a.m. We needed enough time to get to the lake at Gyékényes from Csokonyavisonta, which was about 35 miles away. I made sure all my things were neatly organized, went through all the lists in my head,

Confessions of an Ironman

made sure I had everything ready for each of the disciplines, and also made a list of the morning tasks I would need to accomplish. I went to bed at 9:00 p.m.

I managed to sleep about an hour and a half before midnight, but after that I tossed and turned, my mind constantly racing. Everything that could go wrong crossed my mind, including panic during the swim and even possible technical problems on the bike. Physically, I felt prepared. I was fairly confident that I could complete the race, but that was not enough to satisfy me. I kept sizing myself up to my teammates, I wanted to be faster than those I prepared with, and I had specific time expectations, too. Clearly I wanted to finish in under 12 hours. I had a lot to think about and, as I wrote in the introduction, there were many things I came to realize that night. I was actually relieved when the alarm went off because it put a stop to the constant but pointless racing of my thoughts. I had a fixed schedule to follow, and there were no questions in my head anymore. All the things that had filled me with fear the night before would be resolved. There was no plan B. Even if the panic caught up to me, I would still have to get in the water – no one had ever become an Ironman while staying dry. With that said, it would be pointless to continue agonizing. I would work my way through each step, one by one, as they came. It was still early in the morning when I began to slice up the day into tiny steps. First, I would eat my usual, mini scrambled egg breakfast...

After living together for so long, Anikó knew that it was not going to be a morning of cheerful, carefree conversation, and did an outstanding job of handling me. We had one tiny "conflict" in the car on the way to the lake. She assumed I would be happy to listen to some of the motivational music that I played a lot at home, especially since we were headed to the start of my most important race. The truth is, I did not want to hear anything. I just wanted quiet and to sit with my eyes shut. (Fortunately, she was driving.) At one moment I was tense, and in the next second, completely relaxed. Let's get on with it already...

I Knew It Was Well Within My Reach

There Is No Need to Worry About Sleep

When I was doing karate as a child, Mike Tyson was my favorite athlete. The youngest heavyweight boxing champion of the world, he had written in his autobiography that his coach, Cus D'Amato, once told him: "Ninety percent of the fatigue felt in the boxing ring is psychological. It is an excuse used by a man who wants to quit, who wants to get out. You will not be able to sleep before the fight. Do not worry, your opponent has not slept either!"

These thoughts were in complete harmony with everything my more experienced teammates told me during my preparation. Few people sleep well the night before the race. One guy with over 10 Ironman completions under his belt told me he still regularly has nightmares in which he misses the race, arriving on the wrong day. After hearing that story and being overwhelmed with the stress of facing my very first such challenge, I didn't expect a restful night.

The good news, according to the experts, is that it is not about how much you sleep the night before the race, but how much good rest you "collect" during the final week leading up to the race. During the last, and most demanding phase of the preparation, I put in 8 hours a night, as opposed to the usual 5-6. During the last, tapering week, I slept as much as 9-10 hours a night.

THE LONGEST DAY

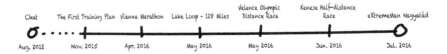

When we arrived at Gyékényes, I quickly removed the bike from the roof rack, checked it over for the one-hundredth time to make sure that everything was nicely in place, and was off to check in. My nerves were so high-strung that I managed to lose one of my bike gloves in the process – I looked for it for a little while, but since I didn't think it was that important, I decided to go down to the water to wander around with the other competitors.

Earlier, I found this "longest day" expression quite funny since it was only a 12-hour race, as I had told Bence. But since I had been up since midnight, I began to understand the meaning behind the phrase. My mind had finally stopped racing. I was able to calm down and collect myself by applying the same technique I used at the Budapest half-distance race: I broke the process down into tiny pieces and shut out everything but the very next small step, which was always simple enough that I didn't really have anything to worry about. My first task was to find a suitable start position in the crowd for the hour-and-a-half swim pace I had made plans for, making sure I was far enough to the side so that I could begin my strokes undisturbed – relative to the circumstances – once some space opened up in front of me. This seemed manageable, and I didn't think further ahead.

The Longest Day

When they began playing those signature songs which traditionally signaled that it was nearly time for the start, I found a spot in the crowd which seemed ideal and just waited. It did wonders to the tension of the moment that Anikó was standing only a few yards away, crying among the spectators. First, I made an attempt to comfort her, telling her that everything was going to be just perfect. When I noticed that some photographers, who initially got closer to take pictures of the athletes, ended up taking pictures of her instead as they were moved by her tears, I left her with it, giving the "reporters" a smile.

At that point. I didn't feel any kind of fear. "I am not here to try to do an Ironman," I thought. "I am here because I am going to do one." My trademark – the complete absence of a plan B – was great in making the situation as straightforward as it could be, leaving no room for any worrying at all. I had completed the best possible training plan, I had put in the necessary work, and waiting for the perfect moment – no matter what the life situation, I think – is useless, as it will never come. One simply has to be brave enough to take a leap and dive into the adventure without leaving any doors open to turn back; the experience of a lifetime will be guaranteed. (That is how I started my own business and that is how I became an investor also – why would I have changed a proven recipe?) I am not a *Star Wars* fanatic, but I have to admit that Yoda's phrase "Do or do not. There is no try." resonates with me! Similar to this is a thought from Bodo Schaefer's audiobook, which I listened to on my runs, that "those who experiment are simply in search of obstacles to stumble over." I did not achieve financial freedom around the age of 33 with an "I'll give it a try and see if it works" attitude, either. I would have had countless reasons to turn back, deterred by the great many slaps I have gotten in my face while on that road. One needs solid determination to achieve a greater goal, it is not enough to simply try. I am not an experimenter, I came here to go all the way! I would have plenty of time later to deal with my thoughts from the previous night, because I will definitely have something to do with them.

The Rocking Chair Test

This is an interesting "technique" which can be very useful in situations when you tense up, troubled by a decision you need to make, and are filled with uncertainty. It can simplify the process beyond belief if you picture yourself old, sitting on your porch in a rocking chair, asking yourself the question: "Looking back at your life, would you regret not doing this thing?" If you feel that the answer might be yes, you should definitely jump right in!

Are the circumstances not ideal? Let me spare you the suspense – they will never be. Successful people do not hesitate to take the first step toward their goal, even in less than ideal situations. It might very well be that you do not see a perfect reasoning behind what you are about to do – like I did not see it in the Ironman project – but the rocking chair test still told me that I should do it. Trust your feelings when they tell you that you'd regret it if you did not do it! Not everything has to make perfect sense in the beginning.

The following thought could open a door to some invaluable realizations if you take a moment to recall events from your own life, which stand proof that it is true: **Life can only be understood backwards, but it must be lived forwards.** *I Can See Clearly Now*, one of Dr. Wayne Dyer's books, is about that. It puts in focus that when we look back at a given event of our lives – which, at that time, we may have seen as unfortunate for some reason – the puzzle pieces will begin to find their places and the resulting picture will reveal why things had to happen the way that they did. If you think about it, this kind of book could be written about any one of us. This message is in perfect harmony with the philosophy of Zen, or with the Nike slogan (whichever you're comfortable with): Just do it!

The Longest Day

The cannon was fired! I quickly hit the "Start" button on my watch while many others charged into the water. I was not rushing, I was taking my time to find my place on the side. I reached the water, and I was still just walking, looking for the ideal "lane". There is actually a recording of me as I was looking around, standing up, while most everyone else was already swimming. I knew that no matter how much time I'd lose waiting, I would make it up exponentially if I could manage to get through the swim without any panic. The moment finally came when I could get on my way, and the next step was to get to the first buoy, swimming as easily and as calmly as I could. It might be because I simply couldn't afford it at this race, or maybe because the water was beautifully clear and I could see all my fellow competitors and could avoid the majority of the kicks and punches, but I did not feel the slightest trace of fear. Slowly but surely, I moved along, feeling very comfortable. I kept passing those around me, and I always managed to position myself in a way which enabled me to swim without any major obstacles – although it did not seem like an easy thing to achieve once about 700 athletes began swimming in a mass start.

It was a two-lap swim course. The only challenge I foresaw in the first discipline was that I might have to overcome a possible panic attack, but since it seemed to have taken a day off, I was almost certain I would easily be able to achieve the previously planned sub hour-and-a-half swim time. At the end of the first lap, we had to leave the water and run about 30-40 yards as we turned around for the second lap. I had a chance to glance at my watch and saw that I was inside 40 minutes after the first 1900 meters (1.2 miles), which was way better than expected. On the second lap, some teammates who were better swimmers caught up and passed me, not surprisingly. By that time, though, I considered the swim a done deal and I was already thinking about the next small step, the first transition: In what order I'd be doing things, and that I would be sure to put on my compression socks which I had neatly set out next to the bike.

Confessions of an Ironman

I did such a great job occupying myself with these thoughts that in the next moment I realized I was right near the shore and that it was almost time to get out of the water. My swim time was 1 hour 19 minutes, which meant that, even if I was super slow in transition, I was still well on schedule to get on the road within an hour and a half. Everything was going as planned – actually, even better.

I spent less than 5 minutes in the transition area. I could have used a bathroom break, but since I did not see any nearby, I decided not to waste time with it. I pushed my bike to the mount line, I waved to Anikó and my family, and I began the most crucial part of the race. I built a 10-minute advantage in the swim, and 5 more with my transition, relative to the time I had made plans for, so the next goal was to complete the bike course inside 6 hours. I felt very well, the swim did not take anything out of me, and I was ready for the cycling challenge.

Since I was familiar with the course, thanks to my earlier weekend testing, I knew that the first section was the more difficult one. It was hillier and the road quality was not the best. During one of the final practice sessions Ákos told me that I should be fine doing around 19-20 mph, but a ~21 mph pace would be too fast to maintain the whole way. His words were ringing in my head when I was doing a speed that "would be too fast to maintain the whole way." The first part of the bike course took us through some really beautiful landscape. I had plenty of energy, which made it very easy to lose my focus and push a bit harder than reasonable. I didn't get myself into trouble, though, as my watch kept me in check and reminded me to slow down. As I got more tired, it felt natural to keep my speed around 19 mph.

My calculations predicted a near 6-hour bike ride and I celebrated each passing mile because they got me closer and closer to the end of the second act. (And perhaps to the end of the last long bike ride of my life, because that sport did not make it onto my favorites list.) I had a lot of time to think in the saddle, too.

The Longest Day

It got very warm fairly quickly, so my three bottle set-up proved to be a very good decision because that way, from one aid station to the next, I could drink about half of the water and was also able to cool my body with the rest by pouring it all over me. I took a drink from the lighter gel solution every half hour as planned, I followed it with water, and sipped on some isotonic beverage whenever I felt I needed it. I was hopeful that my nutrition plan was going to work, and there was enough gel in my bottle, even with the last-minute change.

I passed one of my teammates as early as the forest road in the very first section of the bike course while he was getting rid of some *ballast*. We cheerfully waved at each other. The truth is, I could have used a pit stop myself, since I couldn't find a toilet after the swim. I didn't feel any immediate danger at that point, so I passed on it once again. It was very interesting to find that the thoughts and feelings which had haunted me throughout the night returned during the race. Instead of focusing on myself, I kept wondering where my teammates might be at any given moment, when they would pass me, where we would meet again. There they were again, those self-comparisons.

I Am Not in It for the Ranking, But...

Many people say they are not out there to chase a specific finish time or a certain ranking, but simply for the pleasure of the sport. I feel the same way, theoretically, but the first thing I do after I cross the finish line is look at my time and, as soon as I can, find out where my given day's performance put me in the field. I still find it challenging to resist making constant calculations in those areas of life where, similar to sports, accomplishments are measurable, where one can keep score.

Once the performance is complete, then it can easily be compared with internal or external expectations, and even with the results of others. This process – if done without control – can actually take the pleasure out of the entire experience. It would be wise to keep that in mind.

Confessions of an Ironman

I made my way through the first 46-mile section of the course, from Gyékényes to Nagyatád, where Anikó was waiting for my arrival. We saw each other, she waved to me, but the rest of the family missed me. I was way ahead of schedule, but there was still a whole lot of racing to be done. The rest of the bike course consisted of three "small" approximately 22-mile loops, which I was not looking forward to at all. Somewhere around mile 56, I arrived at an aid station, but before I got there, as sort of a routine, I dumped the left-over water on me from the designated bottle and only tossed it after it was empty, so as to make room for the new load. I reached out to pick up the new bottle from a volunteer and slung it behind me into the right-side slot of the bottle holder behind my saddle. (The other one, on the left side, contained my emergency kit, complete with tools, CO_2 canisters, and inner tubes. I was terrified that I might have to use them – nevertheless I was prepared for the worst. I even taped up a couple of extra inner tubes onto my bike frame, along with additional energy bars, which I actually ate during the ride.)

Just as I was leaving the aid station behind, I glanced at my watch and saw that it was time for the next gulps from the gel mix, and no matter how nauseating that tutti-frutti-tasting substance felt by then, I still had to force it down and chase it with a lot of water so that it would not turn into "deadly poison" in my body. Every single time I took a drink, Gábor Kindl's words rang in my ears. This time though, I had a different problem. As I reached back for the water, I could not find anything, no matter how hard I tried; the bottle I had just picked up a few minutes earlier was not there. I looked back and saw that one of the screws that held the right-side bottle holder in place had gotten loose, and my water bottle was dangling upside down. At that point, my challenge wasn't only that it required a magic trick to get it to slide out of that unnatural position so that I could finally get a drink, but, what's way worse, I was there with 2 bottle holders and 3 bottles, which seemed less than ideal for the remaining 56 miles.

I had to get rid of one of the bottles and carry on with only two. The gel mix was a keeper because without that I would not stand

The Longest Day

a chance. I also needed water to drink with the gel mix, plus to cool my body in the roughly 90-degree heat; I parted ways with the isotonic drink. That single bottle of water now had to supply me with enough liquid to chase the gel mix and to cool myself. As it turned out, that was simply impossible – I kept running out of water before I could replenish my supplies, which meant that I couldn't even use the gel mix as planned, or rather I did not want to risk using it. I did not put as much gel in it to start with and I was in a situation where I was afraid to drink even that. I knew that my nutrition plan may not suffice, and I began to feel that with each passing mile.

My attention was on my teammates at each turnaround point to see where they were relative to me, and on my speedometer in an attempt to keep my tempo around the 19 mph, which proved to be more and more difficult. The "time-advantage" I built in the beginning of the bike leg with my faster than expected start came in very handy; I managed to complete the bike course in 5 hours and 54 minutes.

Over the last two "small laps" I got fairly close to István Kovács (Kokó), an Olympic and professional world champion boxer from Hungary, who has fallen in love with the sport of triathlon after retiring. It is needless to say how far off I felt from the level of a professional athlete (despite the age difference) whom I had occasionally cheered on while sitting in front of the TV in my high school years, but there we were, rolling along at the same pace. That made me feel very good and I thought I was doing pretty well, considering I was nearing the end of the bike leg.

As I got into transition, the following thoughts ensued: I would not miss biking for a long time, I need some time to get used to walking again (but a marathon would surely provide me with plenty enough of that), and it was high time for the bathroom break I had been putting off for the good part of six hours. Some even took a shower and changed before the run, but I did it all wearing my singlet over my swim trunks.

I changed my shoes and began my stumble onto the run course. Anikó called me from behind a fence and asked me if she could

Confessions of an Ironman

help me with anything. What she meant was if she could give me anything from the carefully assembled nutrition pack which she had with her in case I would need anything to keep me alive. All I could answer, with a smile nailed onto my face, was "Take half of the run for me." I'm sure this made it clear to her that this marathon was not going to be the most pleasant experience of my life.

I glanced at my watch at the beginning of the run and saw that in the event I survived the remaining 26.2 miles, it was almost certain that I would finish with a time inside 12 hours. I had gained 6 more minutes over my planned time with my bike and 5 more minutes during that last transition – I had an almost half-hour "advantage." From that point on, technical problems were ruled out, leaving only me and my perseverance in the equation. Still, the remaining distance was much more than my brain could fathom. It was especially fortunate that the run course winding through town consisted of eight loops. I focused on one lap at a time, and within each one, I solely concentrated on reaching the very next aid station, which was all the more important because, by that time, the heat grew extreme and I constantly needed to cool my body with water.

Despite having some experience, I still managed to make a mistake: As I dumped the water all over myself to keep cool, I completely drenched my shoes. The result of which is usually that my toenails turn black and fall off, and that is not a good way to run.

I had always gone out fast after the bike and it was no different in Nagyatád. I had to consciously hold myself back, all the way until it became automatic as my fatigue grew. I was able to run 6 miles at a sub 9:40 pace, but in the third lap I started to feel that I would not be able to keep that up and that I needed to get something in me even though I couldn't even look at the gels and energy bars anymore. I managed to force down a salty energy bar and actually felt its positive effects, because I could get back up to the 9:40 pace after I ate it. With that, halfway through the run, I was beginning to feel convinced that if I survived the second half of the marathon,

The Longest Day

even if my run time ended up slower than I had planned, my overall time would surely be inside 12 hours. All I had left were four more laps and I would accomplish my most daring goal.

Some of my teammates were running with huge grins on their faces, while I was in a totally different state. We watched one another at each turnaround, and after some time I began to notice that our countenances slowly began to look more alike – needless to say, this was not induced by my changing to a cheerier mode.

The final laps perfectly exemplified how I am not the competitive athlete type. As soon as I saw that my goal was within reach, and as it also became more and more apparent that those teammates of mine whom I prepared with were not going to pass me, I stopped putting effort into pushing myself further. My splits were banging the doors of eleven-minute miles, I was clearly in great need of some more gels or energy bars because I was getting destroyed, and still I made a perfectly conscious decision that I'd rather finish slower, but I would not eat any more of those things. So much for maximalism.

Anikó and the others were there for me at each lap, waiting in the park that was part of the run course which also provided some much needed shade at every lap. They asked what they could get me from the well-equipped aid pack, but I only asked for tomatoes because it felt good to chew on those. The last 6-9 miles were all about will power. I think most would have stopped for a while in that state, but I don't do that; a few minutes would not recharge me, and the distance does not get less while I am standing around. I always say "let's get going, because this thing will not run itself," which many people smile about but I mean wholeheartedly. I only stop when I cross the finish line. Taking a break before that is useless, it will only make the suffering last longer.

When I turned onto the final lap, I did pause for a bit to stretch out my thighs, but a few steps later they felt just as heavy as before. I think that this part, which is all about will power and suffering, is an

Confessions of an Ironman

essential element of this race; it is what enables me to truly value the result. Finishing without that pain would leave me with a void and it is likely that I would start toying with the idea of a double Ironman...

On my last lap, I politely said my farewells to all the volunteers counting the completed laps on the other side of the run course. I thanked them for their work and although I was beginning my final miles, I kept on plugging away at the same pace. I even picked up some Coke and crackers at one of the aid stations, despite the fact that they had never worked for me. At that point, I allowed myself to make a deviation from my "safe-zone" of sports foods and go for the enjoyment.

Just as I was battling to keep my unplanned "snacks" down until the finish, a speaker in the shaded park called on me and told me I ought to smile for him as I was about two-thirds of a mile away from completing the very first Ironman triathlon of my life. Looking back at the pictures taken during the run, I couldn't say that my face reflected carefree joy. Anikó was entrusted with the task to periodically send word home to my mom, reporting whether I was still alive, since she could not make it to the race. Later they told me that even though they used three different phones to take pictures, most of the shots did not make it into the send box because they felt "she cannot see him like that."

By then, it was obvious that my marathon time would be outside four hours. It was also quite certain that my overall time would be over 11 and a half. I had accepted that, as there was nothing I could do to change it. As I made my final turn onto the finishing stretch, I heard the main speaker say what I had heard a hundred times before in my head: "Dávid Sólyomi, you are an Ironman," and he added, "representing Team Megathlon." The latter surprised me, because I had never considered myself to be at a level where I could be regarded as an athlete who is part of a sports team. I simply did not consider myself good enough for that. On the other hand, the "Dávid Sólyomi, you are an Ironman" greeting I had lived through several times during a sort of relaxation exercise that I learned at the Silva Mind Control Method training and kept practicing almost every evening. I can honestly say that the live experience was not much different or any more intensified.

At the mind control training, I learned how to put myself in an alpha state so that I could visualize certain experiences. I cannot say that I was in a completely relaxed state each time, neither did I take all elements of those exercises entirely seriously, but I did go through the full race, from start to finish, almost every night before I fell asleep. Seeing those images more and more, and with the progress I was making in my preparation, it grew very clear and unquestionable in me that I would complete this race.

Don't get me wrong, it felt great to hear that I was an Ironman, but I still was not done; I had to give Anikó the rose of gratitude I was given running down the last meters (it is a custom at the Nagyatád race that each athlete who is about to cross the finish line is handed a rose that they can keep or give anyone they wish). I also had to receive the finisher medal and finally the finisher T-shirt. I crossed the finish line, holding the tape and the rose, but I could not find the person the flower belonged to, so I eloquently posed an inquiry looking at my other family members. My simple "Where is she?" came out with such intonation that we still laugh about it when we listen to it thanks to a short video made using a phone. Besides my broken bottle holder, that was the part that did not go as I had planned, because the man standing in front of me who was handing out the medals got tired of waiting and asked me to take the finisher medal and told me I could do whatever I wanted with the flower afterwards. It was not the order I visualized, but I was even more disappointed with the quality of the T-shirt, which was supposed to represent a significant memory for an individual finisher of a long-distance triathlon race.

Despite the fact that I am an admittedly "overcompensating medal collector" and I like these sorts of souvenirs, I did not let the subpar quality of the finisher medal or the T-shirt spoil my mood. I hope

Confessions of an Ironman

those in charge will put more emphasis on these elements in the future because, besides that, I think they put together a well-organized race with an amazing atmosphere.

After making my rounds with the family, I walked into the massage tent in the finishers' area, where I was told that I didn't even look like I had just completed an Ironman. I needed to wait until they took care of those seemingly in greater need of help who had almost died completing the same stunt. A little while later I did get my turn. By that time some of my teammates had also finished and we quickly congratulated each other even before the awards ceremony that was to come later the next day.

I ended up with a 4-hour 10-minute marathon, which, in and of itself, would have been a disappointment. I was far from a mood where I could see anything in a negative light, because my overall race time was 11 hours and 33 minutes, surpassing even my wildest aspirations. I experienced a level of satisfaction like never before. That was the first time when I honestly felt that I did not need to push myself further toward an even greater and more difficult performance, because the Ironman was perfectly enough for me. Many people had told me about similar feelings when talking about their finish, but then I was still very far from being able to imagine my own completion of the Ironman, let alone being able to feel that a given performance could possibly satisfy me to a level where I could stop pushing myself further.

I felt such relief as I crossed the finish line, as if a great weight that had been chained to my leg had been cut off. It represented my basic fear of "I am not good enough" in the realm of manhood. If there is anyone who thinks I am not good enough now, they can go ahead and do it after me! What's even more important, parallel to my physical preparation, my adventure of self-discovery led me to where I feel good, regardless of what others think, and I accept myself for who I am. This gives me a sense of freedom I have never felt before.

How Many Bags Have You Put Down, and How Many Are You Still Carrying?

I was thirty-four when I crossed the finish line of the Ironman. By then, I felt I had been able to put down two extremely heavy bags: One was connected to money and breaking free of the modern slavery of employment, and the other to the feeling of "I am not good enough" in the dimension of my physical body, my manhood.

Undoubtedly, I was the one who once decided to pick up and carry these heavy loads. However, those decisions were not made on a conscious level, which is why it took long years of difficult self-exploration before I realized that I was trying to move forward in my life with (at least) two immense burdens weighing me down, and that my journey could become much easier without them.

I have made my fair share of investments in my life – as it happens to be my passion – and I can wholeheartedly say that the greatest return came from the work that I have invested in myself, the countless seminars, and the constant reading. Having read this far, if you feel that I could help you on your journey of self-discovery or with any of your specific goals, feel free to check my calendar and schedule a coaching call at davidsolyomi.com.

The "longest day" slogan revealed its true meaning to me when, following a quick meal after the race, we got home and went out to dinner. Bence was very cute when he went to great lengths to convince me that I should have an ice cream and, just so that I wouldn't feel alone, he would join me and consume his thirtieth portion of sweets that day. What else could one have done while waiting around for the end of a "twelve-hour race" hanging out by those outdoor pools in Nagyatád.

WHAT ABOUT THE PAPER?

I had thought I would finally get some good sleep before the awards ceremony the next day, where I would receive the certificate of completion, which is what I came for in the first place. After the disappointment in the quality of the medal and the T-shirt, I was hoping that the certificate would be the same as in previous years.

It was a fine plan, but the reality was that my mind kept spinning, and I could hardly sleep. It was right around 4:00 a.m. when I got tired of myself, and since I figured it wouldn't be very nice of me to wake Anikó, I went outside. Since everyone was sleeping, I thought I'd start loading the trunk with some bike parts, remove the front wheel and the extra inner tubes from the frame, and while I was at it, I would put the bike on the roof rack, too. To my great surprise, when I stepped outside, I was not alone in the yard!

One of my fellow competitors was going through some motions similar to what I had just conjured up, so we struck up a conversation while packing. He told me that he had done many Ironman triathlons, and due to the lack of time to prepare, having kids and all, he relied on the base he had built. His best time was around 12 and a half hours. We shook hands, and he added that my 11 hours and 33 minutes could only come with the kind of training program I had gone through, and if down the line I won't be able to train as much, I should let go of those sorts of results and be ready to find pleasure in simply completing the distance because that also has its own beauty.

What About the Paper?

The awards ceremony was held in the City Sports Hall in Nagyatád, where the competitors had designated seats based on their finishing times. Since I came in 134th out of 601 individual finishers, my spot was fairly close to the front. So close, actually, that I could hardly find it, and in the midst of my search I even got a little worked up because, as I was looking around, I saw the certificates with the finish line photos and time splits on every chair around me, but mine was nowhere to be found. I didn't hesitate and quickly asked an organizer what the deal was, which is when I learned that the first-time finishers would be presented with their diplomas later, on stage. This was not new information, I had simply forgotten, plus there weren't really any seats around me without a certificate. Most "rookies" do not finish with that kind of time, which I also heard from a four-time finisher sitting next to me, while on my other side, there was Kokó, the professional boxer, who had just completed his second Ironman with a time one minute faster than mine.

The certificate did not turn out to be a disappointment, but the ceremony stretched so long that I could not contain myself and made a sacrifice on the altar of "self-display" by posting a picture of it on Facebook. Everyone around me was doing the same, so it would have been very difficult to resist. From that point on, I could occupy myself with counting how many *likes* and congratulating comments I received. I was content, but it was not because of any external factors; those simply served as extra icing on the cake, at best.

Following the race, I was free from the rigorous training program which had previously filled my weeks, and I made rest my focus. I recall how relaxed I was while walking (with hardly any toenails) to the office to scan my certificate so that I could have a digital copy of it before putting it in a frame. It is seldom that I am not in a hurry and nothing around me needs special attention, so it was a strange but also very pleasant feeling. I knew a framer – he had done some very professional work for me with valuable, antique Rockefeller shares and hyperinflation bills – so when I put the certificate in

Confessions of an Ironman

front of him and he saw the figures on it, he said that it looked like I worked a long time to earn it and he would make sure to do a good job. As he tried to decipher what sports I had done, over what distances and how long, he made a comment saying that it had to have been a multi-day thing, right? After I clarified it for him, he made the following, curious remark as I was leaving, "I had no idea there were people who did that sort of thing."

This made me think, as I was sitting on the tram on the way home, that people, in general, do not do *that sort of thing*. They just don't, because it takes a clear sense of purpose, perseverance, and the willingness to make a whole lot of sacrifices, all at the same time. Most people don't even have a fraction of these qualities, and if they do, they never manifest because they get suppressed. These people get stuck in situations in which they are not happy, and, as a direct result of their own self-defense mechanisms, rarely admit that to themselves. Countless people hate their jobs, are dissatisfied with their relationships, act helpless while watching their own bellies grow... but as long as they don't talk about it and ignore those thoughts and surround themselves with people who are in the same situation, it doesn't hurt them so much. If only they could avoid those occasional encounters with people who have actually taken responsibility – for themselves, as a matter of fact – and, as a result, are living a completely different life today! This contrast is just too much to handle. It can inflict significant pain – pain so immense that it can even lead to the disillusion of friendships.

There Are Two Roads and It Is Your Choice Which One You Take

I learned many things about, and from, those around me during the many months of the Ironman preparation. It became evident as my training progressed that there were people who felt they were lesser when they saw my progression towards my

What About the Paper?

goal. These individuals were dissatisfied with certain aspects of their own lives and were simply frustrated that I was doing an Ironman while they weren't doing anything.

It is not that they also aspired to achieve a similar athletic performance – something completely different may have been behind those disturbing feelings. There must have been a time when these people, too, had dreams and goals, but they were too lazy to pursue them. They gave up the fight, and have forgotten how to dream. The fault certainly does not lie with the person who has come into their scope, living a different life, reaching various goals; the only "sin" that person might have committed is that he opened their eyes to the fact that life can be lived a different way, too. Some answer this realization with frustration; others may get inspired to make a change, because it is never too late to start living differently.

People were also profoundly shocked when I stood up to teach how it was possible to acquire a steadily growing passive income in the form of dividends by investing in the shares of stable, global companies and how to attain financial freedom. I was the first person to teach this in my country, not to mention that my suggestion was that it could be done without constantly sitting in front of the computer, worrying about the fluctuation of share prices. In the meantime, based on the sales figures and the volume of questions received about my book *Living Free Off of Dividends*,[14] many thousands have gotten over their initial shock, did some reading, learned, and have begun their journey toward their financial goals using a proven recipe.

Like everyone else, you also have two roads to choose from: You can give up on your dreams and bury them somewhere deep, or you can live boldly, being open about what you want, and pursue it wholeheartedly. It is your decision, no one else can make it for you, nor is anyone entitled to cast any judgment,

---

[14] Published in Hungarian in 2015.

Confessions of an Ironman

> regardless of the direction you take. With that said, those who opt for comfortable idling should accept it if someone in their circle chooses the other route and, for instance, decides to prepare for an Ironman. If seeing such "freaks" pains you, then you can at least be grateful to them because they show you that you might have given up something you shouldn't have. This is worth giving some thought because you always have a choice. It's never too late to pick the other road.

The physical aspect of the Ironman was only over for me when I took home my framed certificate and hung it on the wall. But even after that, I had the feeling I would not be done until I took all the notes I had written during my adventures and shaped them into an organized writing from which something could be learned.

WHY DID I DO IT AFTER ALL?

Perhaps it is quite evident by now where my underlying motivation came from. For the onlooker, it is always easier to be wise about others' lives than to clearly see our own. My real motive became clear to me during one of my last runs before the race.

The WHY was not pretty, but I am still going to share it precisely as it revealed itself. I had always been a skinny boy as a child, someone who didn't look muscular and strong. I could never come to terms with that and wanted to become a strong man. As a result, I unconsciously sought out something that seemed to be an outrageously difficult challenge, and which could prove to be enough to make the breakthrough. That is what the Ironman was for me, simply based on its name, without even knowing what it meant or what earning that title required. It doesn't seem to make much sense, does it?

"The rational man, like the Loch Ness monster, is
sighted often but photographed rarely."
David Dreman

I tied my transformation to the Ironman; that is where I was looking for my breakthrough. It was not a conscious choice, but it was beyond any question that I had to go through with it. I did not see any other way, but this was years before the Tony Robbins London event. As it became clear that my constant wrestling was indeed going to take me all the way to the Ironman – as I would not back

Confessions of an Ironman

down until that happened – I began to transform my preparation by making conscious decisions. I set deadlines, and slowly molded the dream into a defined goal. Realizing goals has always been my strong suit.

Naturally, it also helps if you are able to recognize when and how you became programmed with something irrational, which I only came to realize during the years' long project. My enlightenment took a very long time, and was painfully gradual. Subsequently, in light of my ultimate goal, I did recognize the senselessness in wanting to complete an Ironman *(I realized that it was not the Ironman title itself that was going to transform me into a powerful man)*, but my "finish what you started" motivation was much too strong to be able to turn away. When I quit karate, it really left its mark on me. I did not want another similar experience, especially in a domain which I strongly associated with manhood!

I would be curious to find out how many other people were running on the eight lap course at the end of the Ironman with similar, or even wilder motivations. I would be even more interested in knowing how many of them have taken the time to look for the true reasons behind why they were there in the first place. I don't mean those conventional, superficial answers anyone can easily pull out of their sleeves; I mean the real reasons, which are much deeper, and which are often very difficult and uncomfortable to dig up.

The Ironman has given me a lot. It was what I needed to make a breakthrough in the bodily, physical dimension of my life, through which I was able to rid myself of my daunting, compulsive performance anxiety. As a simple country boy who grew up in the lower middle-class suburbs, there were two things I considered impossible: One was that there would come a day when I did not have to work to earn money, and the other was that one day I would be as strong as I perceived others to be. By the time I reached thirty-five, I had managed to put down both of these bags, and that was worth all the work.

Why Did I Do It After All?

My guess is that many people would be frightened of what this freedom means because it provides me with unlimited time; there is nobody to tell me what I have to do with it. The vast majority of people usually don't know how to handle such lack of structure in their day-to-day lives – what's more, it puts them at unease. The countless hours of daily work or the compulsively planned sports activities save them from this unease.

When I first broke free from the office, the sudden freedom shocked me, too. But as time went on, I found my groove in how I structured my time; by now, I love that I can spend my days with activities that I consider to be of value, and through which I can help others. On the other hard, it is not always pleasant to have to think on my own, and to come to certain realizations that can even turn out to be painful. Nonetheless, those who are brave enough to keep going on this journey of self-discovery, which is inexpressibly harder than the Ironman, will not only create a life of superior quality for themselves, but they might also be able to show the way to others. I, for one, love this journey and am glad to share all the knowledge that it provided so that perhaps more people will stand up from behind their desks and dare to dream, and start to live again.

WHAT NOW? THE ROLE OF SPORTS IN MY LIFE

Many people asked me after the Ironman what my next goal would be, how I would continue. Naturally, I asked myself the same questions, even though I had always thought of the project as a one-off, and heading into more extreme directions did not interest me. Finally, I came to the conclusion of "never say never." The Ironman gave me everything I hoped to get from it, which meant there was no *need* to do any more, but since that experience had also indulged me with fantastic adventures, I did not want to go as far as saying that I would never do anything like that ever again. I thought that if I could find the proper motivation and the necessary time, I might find myself behind the starting line again.

I also knew that there needed to be boundaries. They are necessary because most of us tend to go to extremes in those areas of life which can be played for points or results, where success is measurable, and where there is always a higher level to aspire to. Sports and money are perfect examples of this, and in my case, due to the motivations rooted in my childhood, both of these areas were in the spotlight. Of course, there are other things that are also very important, but since they cannot be quantified, they get neglected – human relationships, for instance.

What Now? The Role of Sports in My Life

Uncharted Dimensions

I first heard about this model at one of Ádám Szalay's seminars. It describes the various dimensions of well-being, and states that an individual can only be truly content if none of them are neglected. Since then, I have come across a number of variations on this approach, and based on what I have read, I have made a habit of connecting a specific goal to each of the following dimensions each time I sit down to set my yearly goals.

- I (self-realization): e.g., I will write a book.
- Money: e.g., I will launch my international newsletter service on stock investing.[15]
- Body (this is where all the sports goals can be listed): e.g., I will run at least one marathon next year.
- Nature: e.g., During my months-long world travel, I will detach myself from the urban environment, and I will try what it's like to swim with dolphins.
- Physical Environment: e.g., I will seek out my new home.
- Network (more distant, professional relationships): I will meet at least one person each month from whom I can learn something.
- Relationships: This is where any intimate or closer family relationships belong.
- Spirituality: To avoid any misunderstandings, let me elaborate on this one...

To me, spirituality does not mean praying all day long to an old, bearded man and waiting for abundance to fall into my lap, all while doing nothing. On the other hand, when we reach a certain age, it is inevitable that we start pondering the reasons

---

[15] Launched in 2017 at thefalconmethod.com

for our existence. When our bank accounts or medal displays are filled, most of us realize that there has to be more to life.

When I was first confronted with all these areas, I came to the realization that I had never articulated any goals beyond the dimensions of money and the physical body. No wonder, as these are classic "measured by points" areas of life. I had fallen into the usual trap of concentrating all my energies on those, neglecting the other, less measurable dimensions.

Everyone's day consists of 24 hours. If we overemphasize one area, we can only do so at the expense of another. Clearly, I could easily set a goal to become a twenty-time Ironman finisher, but the question is whether it is worth the sacrifice. According to my current value system, it is not. Dávid Verrasztó, a Hungarian Olympic swimmer, once said in an interview that he questions whether it was a good decision on his part to put all his time and efforts into sports, because, as he said, with his ability to swim from point A to point B in x amount of time he did not create any value. These are his words, not mine! In light of that, what value has my 134th place delivered to the world? This book, at best.

Nonetheless, my little project had its place in my life. It demanded vast amounts of time, and while being fully occupied with it, I did not have to deal with those much more distressing questions (the other dimensions). From the outside, my adventure might have looked to be a kind of escape, an avoidance; but in the end, I gained a lot from it.

It is usually people who are left with no option that end up having to deal with the really important and worthwhile questions; perhaps because they are losing everything or as a result of an accident or an illness are left with no other choice, but to wake up and – using a more fashionable term – become enlightened. Without any external forces, by their own will, few people undertake the difficult task of facing themselves; instead, many of us choose to flee throughout

What Now? The Role of Sports in My Life

our entire lives, chasing goals spewed from the materialistic dimensions, which are forced upon us by social conventions.[16]

I am certain that if I had spent those months devoted to the preparations for the Nagyatád Ironman sipping wine with my friends instead, I would have gained far fewer memorable moments. I think the key lies in finding the balance: I would like to live an adventurous life, filled with great experiences, but I also want to leave something valuable behind for other generations that follow. I will always need a challenge – without that, even an amoeba cannot make it – but I strive for a healthy balance between creating value and indulging in pleasure. From this point on, the possibilities are wide open. Being active in sports, as a means to maintain my health, will always be part of my life, no question about that.

---

[16] John Ortberg's *When the Game Is Over, It All Goes Back in the Box* is an interesting read on the topic.

IV. BONUS ROUND

IRONMAN BARCELONA, HERE I COME!

After the race in Nagyatád, as a sort of a "cooldown," I ran a marathon in Athens in November, without any specific preparation. I was drawn to the race because the course took us from the site of the Battle of Marathon into the Olympic Stadium in Athens, plus their finisher medal looked great. I have always thought of that event as the "authentic" marathon. My plans after that included nothing but rest. The year 2017 was mainly about traveling, and I was certain I wouldn't do any triathlons that year.

I packed my running shoes when we flew to Portugal, and I had them with me when we traveled around in the USA. During that three-four month period, I did not get involved in any regular sports activities. When we got home, I mercilessly shocked my body by returning to the swim- and running practices at the triathlon club. I made sure that everyone knew I did not want anything to do with the bike, which meant that my 2017 season could only include some marathons, at best.

When the day of the 2017 Nagyatád Ironman came, I was lying on a deck chair by Lake Balaton, sipping beer with some of my friends. As I was following the race on my phone to see how my teammates were doing, my thoughts started racing again. *I should be there! I really want to re-live the experience of completing an Ironman. Now, I know what I am up against, I know how much time and work it takes*

Ironman Barcelona, Here I Come!

to get that feeling in return, and I still want it! When we got home the next day, I dusted off my bike, which I had not touched for a full year, mounted it on the home trainer, and spun for an hour. It was decided: I would do an Ironman in 2018.

I did not hesitate to share my wonderful plan with Ákos: In October of 2017, I would run the Frankfurt marathon; in November, I'd run the one in Florence. After that, we could get on with the preparation for an Ironman in 2018, the location of which I would identify in due time. Both marathons left deep impressions. The training period before Frankfurt was very tight, plus I also missed the foundation-building phase at the beginning of the year due to those months of traveling; thanks to my poorly chosen pace, I had to fight for my life to finish in 3 hours and 40 minutes. I only had a few weeks before Florence, but Ákos had a good idea about what we had done wrong in my preparation and turned it all around in such masterful ways that I clocked 3 hours and 19 minutes, my personal best up to that point. What's more, I did not even have to empty my tanks for that result, and felt great when I crossed the finish line. The weather also factored into my quick time; it began pouring right at the start, making me want to get through the race as quickly as possible.

For my second full-distance triathlon, I wanted to pick an event with an Ironman logo stamped on it. If I was going to go through the proper preparation again, I really should have a medal like that in my collection. A lot of people I knew had only good things to say about the Barcelona race. They liked the atmosphere, and said the course was quick, too. The bike leg was allegedly flat, which was very important to me as the second discipline was still not my strong suit. As soon as the registration opened, I signed up for Ironman Barcelona, scheduled to take place on October 7, 2018.

The preparation was incomparable to two years earlier. I felt no pressure whatsoever. I knew I was doing it all for myself, of my own free will, and I was not driven by a desire to prove anything or to live up to any external expectations. This is the only way it makes sense to do sports, but I needed to go through the first Ironman

Confessions of an Ironman

adventure to realize this. Each time I went out, it was great to feel I had put down a tremendous load in that dimension of my life.

The training was always adjusted to be in tune with my current performance level, and my continuous progress was clearly detectable. My plans for before Barcelona, in order to beef up my less than massive triathlon experience, included three half-distance races, one Olympic distance race, and a relay in Nagyatád.

I did the Kenese half-distance race (on a shorter, poorly measured course) in 4 hours and 57 minutes, and later in Tata – which is a small town not too far from Budapest – I managed to finish in 5 hours and 7 minutes, despite a scorching run, on an accurately measured course. These results were very promising, but what's even more important, I was able to enjoy these races and got so comfortable with the half distance that I did not even lose sleep over them. I had reached a completely different level compared to where I was before the long-distance race two years earlier, and had even gotten my hands on a carbon fiber bike. (I felt it would be too big a leap to switch to a time-trial machine, so I stayed with the traditional road bike. I was completely satisfied with my purchase, which had been made with professional help.)

There was one point during the preparation when I had to signal Ákos that it was getting to be a little too much, and that I would not be able to take on more. My international business, which I had launched in the interim, needed my attention. It was reassuring when he told me we were right up to our longest week with over 20 hours of training and would not go beyond that. It goes without saying that there were several sessions throughout the year when I had to get out of my comfort zone. I also got into the saddle for long rides with my teammates, but the workload only became difficult to manage with race day already in close proximity. (Two years earlier, when preparing for Nagyatád, I had to stretch my boundaries almost every day.)

CONTRAST: THE NIGHT BEFORE THE RACE

The technical meeting was on Friday before the Sunday race, so I sat in to gather some useful information, and to get an even better feel for the course. It really knocked my wind out when I heard the speaker say that the "large number of Irish athletes had brought some weather along with them for race day." It hadn't crossed my mind that I might have to battle other things besides the winds coming off the sea, and I certainly did not consider that rain could actually be in the picture. Having arrived early, I did get a chance to see both faces of the place, where one time the gusts almost blew me and my bike off the road, and at another time I could speed down the pavement without any problem. While I knew I could be faced with a wide variety of challenges, rain was certainly not on my list.

I was really surprised that I could sleep the night before the race. I had grown into the Ironman role and my "I don't belong here" feeling had completely vanished; that feeling had probably been the greatest source of my stress back then. "I have already done this before, and now, by any objective measure, I am much better prepared. I am better than at least half the field, so it is beyond any doubt that I DO BELONG HERE." I woke a few times during the night, but all in all, I was able to sleep about 5-6 hours, which is great for a night before an Ironman.

Confessions of an Ironman

During the night, I could hear that the storm had arrived. There was thunder and lightning, and naturally, it was pouring rain. I thought to myself, "It is so unfair that, after so much preparation, I will not be able to go faster than before, simply because of the circumstances... and I have taken so much time away from my family in the process." Come to think of it, is there such a thing as "fair"? "Whatever is to come tomorrow, let it come," I thought, and went back to sleep. I woke up around 4:30 a.m., beating the alarm I had set for 4:45 a.m. My inner clock had signaled...

THE SECOND "LONGEST DAY"

By morning it became obvious that the weather was not going to be ideal. The rain was relentlessly beating on the roof of the tent that covered the transition area, the waves of the sea were frightening, and the wind was blowing hard. Lightning bolts also appeared over the water here and there. I switched to an "I accept what I cannot change" mode and, with that, my feelings took a full turn.

The song *Thunderstruck* from AC/DC was an amusing touch from the organizers. The waves were so enormous that even the professional athletes, who had their own starting time, got tossed around. They were putting in heroic efforts to fight their way through the water, but it seemed as if they were not making any progress. Could the circumstances be any less ideal for a competitor with a fear of water (like me)? There are situations when you cannot rely on anyone to jump in for you to do the job. While it felt reassuring to receive countless messages cheering me on before the race, I also knew that I was the one who would rush into the waves, and others would only think about me from afar. When the time came, I was always on my own.

When it was my turn to start, I looked for a wave that seemed somewhat manageable. (The last two I had seen tossed the swimmers back to shore!) Eventually, I got underway. I quickly settled into a pace that felt comfortable. I had covered the chafing on my neck, which I acquired on Friday while testing the water, with

Confessions of an Ironman

a huge lump of Vaseline, and didn't feel any pain as the wetsuit kept rubbing against the irritated area. Had I used that stuff when I went for the test swim, I wouldn't have had anything to worry about. I was finally able to bust out the Vaseline, which had actually been the butt of some funny jokes back in 2012, as mentioned during the chat which started it all. I had come a long way since then.

I was still within the first 300 yards, and hadn't even reached the first buoy, when I already felt if I could keep away from the kicks and punches, I would be fine all the way through. My initial plan was to be out of the water in around 1 hour and 20 minutes, but I dumped that idea even before the start since I had never attempted to swim among such huge waves. For me, swimming in the sea was not only challenging because I had to battle my general fear of water. I had also always been one of those kids who screamed and puked on roller coasters; my stomach was begging for mercy by the last third of the swim, letting me know it had had enough of the waves. I finally managed to reach the shore without any significant adversities, and my watch showed 1 hour and 11 minutes, which blew my mind. I seriously thought it might have gotten stopped by a kick and then gotten smacked and started again. It was hard to believe that split, but I did not let it puzzle me for long. I hurried to transition instead.

If I could actually believe the watch, I had piled up enough time advantage to allow me to take a quick bathroom break before I hit the bike course. The rain had stopped by the beginning of the bike, and the weather turned favorable. I felt lucky! The bike course was said to be flat and quick, but I think only the latter was true. (My Garmin measured 2950 feet of elevation gain over 113 miles. Flat means something else in my book, but I am sure the professional athletes would see it differently.) I went out very fast, and I followed my nutrition plan to the T, which I had created using the Enduraid mobile application. I hadn't even reached the halfway point when I already had a 15-20-minute advantage racked up, relative to the "19 mph, standard tempo." I had set out for a 5-hour 40-45-minute bike time, so it would have been enough to roll through the second

The Second "Longest Day"

56 miles at around 19 mph. That is when it began to rain like there was no tomorrow, and the winds picked up as well.

At around mile 68, a man, who looked like a spectator, was wildly waving to me to slow down right before a roundabout. I did, but I did not see any roadblocks, and it was not the first time I negotiated a roundabout as the Spanish tend to use them all over the place. The only problem was that there was so much water on the road that my bike slipped from under me as I hit the shoulder board, and I slid on my side all the way to the other side of the lane. I got right up and immediately started to check my bike for damage, completely disregarding my own bloody wounds. Luckily, my body had dampened the blow and I did not see any obvious damage to my bicycle; all I said to the volunteer standing next to me was "I think I am OK." I was then back on my way. Right before the crash, my mind was getting numb from the monotonous pedaling, so, as strange as it may sound, the fall helped shake me up. My legs were getting fatigued, which was another reason to take it somewhat easier. I thought it through and knew that I was primarily there to finish the race; I felt that only a technical problem could prevent me from doing that and it seemed like a good idea to be more careful. The final time would only be decided on the run, and it looked like I was going to get there with a very good split. The only question that remained in my head was whether I would be able to deliver the 8-minute miles I had planned.

Twelve miles from the bike finish, I couldn't even bend down to put my elbows onto the aerobars without pain. I didn't wait until I reached the transition, and stopped for my second bathroom break. (I still don't know how I managed Nagyatád with only one stop.) The truth is, I really needed that short, 1-minute break because I was exhausted. After the pit stop, I got my second wind and was able to complete the remaining distance with a fairly good tempo.

My 5-hour 42-minute bike time was well within my planned limits, and I was also glad because I did not get a penalty. Yellow cards were given all over the course; because there were so many competitors

Confessions of an Ironman

it was very difficult to keep the required distance between riders on a course that had a finite length. Naturally, I did everything I could not to give the officials any reasons to penalize me, so whenever a referee pulled up beside me on a motorbike, I punched it, even when going uphill, so they wouldn't even think about questioning how fast I went past the others. Unlike a massive number of my fellow competitors, I didn't collect any 5-minute penalties. This, by the way, was due to sheer luck. Every yellow card I saw given seemed completely unjustified. The point is, I did not lose any of the advantage I managed to pile up on the bike course because of penalties.

Unfortunately, there were negatives that put their marks on the remainder of the race. I followed the Enduraid mobile app's nutrition advice, but I left out the isotonic drinks. I never drank the full 2 deciliters, which was the prescribed amount, and consumed about half a liter (15 oz) less than I was supposed to during the bike ride. This amount does make a difference, not to mention that I also skipped the last gel before I got into transition because I didn't feel I needed it, and I thought there would be plenty of opportunities on the run to get it on board later. I didn't have to wait long before I felt hungry, which meant that I managed to screw up my nutrition once again, just like in Nagyatád.

My transition felt quick. After changing my shoes, I picked up my nutrition plan notes and salt tablets, and I was off for the marathon. Over the first few miles, I easily managed about a 7:50-mile pace, but my energy levels began to drop much sooner than when the Enduraid plan would have asked me to pop the energy gels. (It was a mistake to skip the last one, scheduled for the end of the bike.) I tried to force myself to keep to the initial plan, but when I slowed to an around 9:40 per mile "crawl," feeling really awful, I began to take things on board as I saw best, which was a risky move. I consumed all kinds of never-before-tested gels (peanut butter flavored, caffeine-rich), salty nuts... you name it. I resurrected myself three times over the whole run, each time bringing my pace back up to around 8:20 per mile from about a 9:40 tempo. I had to play a juggling game as

The Second "Longest Day"

to how much gel my sensitive stomach could still handle, and that became very painful by the end. I remember I saw a billboard by the running course that read "Never trust a fart at an Ironman" which, I am sorry to say, is a very real part of the "atmosphere" on the running course. That far into the Ironman run, most competitors' intestines are rioting against any and all magic potions.

My split was 7 hours and 3 minutes when I began the run. I thought if I could somehow put a 3:30 marathon together, I could finish with a fantastic time around 10:33. But even if I couldn't, I knew I ought to be able to get through the run somewhere inside four hours, and an 11-hour time would still be thirty minutes better than my earlier result. The truth is, I really would have liked to squeeze my time under the 11-hour mark, but it was way too early to think about that at the beginning of the run. Later, I was too preoccupied with the constant need to resuscitate and revive myself. I had to have messed up very badly because there were times I could hardly see and I thought I was going to pass out, even though I drank a lot and took plenty of carbohydrates and salt on board.

I did some math over the last couple of miles and realized that I could get home under 10 hours and 50 minutes if I was able to keep it together, so I made that my goal. I cannot say it was easy, but I did it. The video and the pictures taken at the finish do not really show how destroyed I was, although after crossing the line, I immediately grabbed the rails by the finish area, and then went into the athlete's garden tent and devoured everything I could get my hands on. I was shaking with cold, I was dizzy, but I was proud of my 10:49:13 result. You know what they say: Pain is temporary, pride is forever.

NOW I CAN LET GO

Ákos thought I would have been able to come in at Barcelona around 10:30 under "laboratory circumstances." The waves, the wind, and the rain did not really present the best conditions, and I made it even worse by messing up my nutrition. Despite all that, I am not interested in whether I could go faster in another Ironman, as that would lead to a never-ending spiral. What I hoped to get from this kind of adventure, I did. The second race was only a bonus. I did it for the adventure and for the experience of the carefree enjoyment of sports.

It's been a long journey from that chat about my mother's old bike to the sub 11-hour Ironman completion, but it helped me realize who I am and what my values are. I came to the conclusion that if there is anyone out there who thinks I am not good enough if I don't keep on chasing one Ironman race after another (or any other extreme performance), then there is no room for that person in my life.

There is still one thing I would not say no to for sure: an invitation to the birthplace of the Ironman, to the Hawaii World Championship. After all, the bike course is not new to me at all!

NO EXCUSES!

I am better known for being an investor than for my sports "achievements," but in my immediate circles, the question of how I reached my goals in both areas comes up from time to time. When that happens, I don't usually get very far before the "yes, but..." reactions pop up, which are nothing but personal excuses.

I don't have a problem with that, because I can only talk about what I have gone through, what has been my path. There isn't one universal "happiness and success" recipe! We are all different, and it is not advisable to try copying someone blindly, no matter how successful that person might appear. What motivates me may not move you even one bit. I think the most important thing is to find something that you truly love and for which you are happy to wake up every day. It doesn't matter what that is, because if your drive is rooted in genuine passion, it is certain you will be exceptionally good at it. As for the usual "yes, but..." excuses: They do not work, because there is no limit to what one can do to make a living, as long as they are better at it than most! The person who discovered Justin Bieber, for instance, loved watching YouTube videos. Today, he makes a pretty hefty living doing that.[17]

---

[17] Google "Scooter Braun" for more info.

Is There Life Beyond Painkillers?

Those who work in jobs where they cannot find fulfillment and, without any sense of self-realization or value creation, simply sell their time for compensation, end up needing more money than those who are brave enough to walk their own path. Those belonging to the prior group wind up spending vast sums of money on various painkillers (unnecessary luxury items, endless thrill-seeking, drugs, alcohol, sex, food, etc.), just so that they can suppress the "I don't feel well, my life sucks" feeling. Those whose lives pain them spend way more than those who are ready to tackle each day with a healthy spirit in order to create something that they feel is of value. I know quite a few people who now live off of a fraction of their previous managerial salaries, because they were willing to show who they really are and changed direction.

I am not saying that we should give up money, as it is also an important part of our lives. I agree with Tony Robbins: "Become wealthy, so that you may arrive at your problems in style!" The biggest failure in life, in my opinion, is when someone becomes successful by superficial measures and values (for example, when someone makes a lot of money), but does not attain any sense of accomplishment through the process. To avoid these kinds of "misfortunes" it is important to investigate the reasons why we want to pursue something, to find out the underlying motives so we can make a living doing something that also has a deeper meaning to us.

I was about thirty when I began to realize that making money, in and of itself, was not satisfying enough for me. Today, I see money as a wonderful by-product of creating value. When something leaves my hands that I think is useful and could help others, the money part of the equation usually takes care of itself. On top of that, I am in the fortunate situation of

No Excuses!

having more ideas waiting to be realized than what could fit in a lifetime.

I read a ton of books while I was on my journey of self-development and what dawned on me may cause you to pause and think for a moment, too. As a child, you did not have a problem envisioning yourself as a princess, a ninja, or anything for that matter, and you could even behave like one. You were able to mold that fantasy world into your reality while getting completely immersed in the feelings connected with it. Later, when you reached a certain age, clever adults began to remind you that it was time to start changing and it would be much more useful if you spent your time with things they thought were more sensible, because those were more socially acceptable. You, similar to them, ought to conform to those expectations and become "normal." That is the only way you would be able to get ahead and make money as an adult.

The child, enthused and full of spirit, sees the contrast between his colorful, exciting world and the grey haze that is being forced upon him; still, he accepts what he's shown, and leaves behind what he feels is right, and begins to follow the new direction. Job well done by the parents: Now he is making a great living as a valued member of society, the display could not be more brilliant, all involved deserve a huge pat on the shoulder! The problem is that most of these people feel empty on the inside, and they either seek remedy in spending their money on the previously mentioned "painkillers," or – in more fortunate cases – embark on the painful road of self-discovery, and begin to investigate and learn why the coveted happiness that their parents said would be the fruit of reaching all those goals they worshiped has never come.

No matter how many hundreds of books and seminars I came across on my journey, I felt that when I was a child, almost all of the messages conveyed were totally natural to me! The solutions and "techniques," which are taught for unthinkable amounts of money, we carry within ourselves and instinctively use them from the first moment, until the point when the adults shut those functions down. Later, as we grow into adulthood, after spending fortunes and enduring great pains, we relearn how to live in the moment, how to look at the world around us with genuine enthusiasm (and not the least, how to manifest things with our thoughts, which are filled with very strong emotions). The question then is obvious: If this is the ultimate goal, why is this innate capability torn out of us at the earliest possible moment?

I stumbled upon a story multiple times in seminars and in books. There is an alien who meets a seemingly haggard man sitting on the subway. He asks him:

- Where are you headed?
- I am going to work.
- And why do you do that?
- To make money.
- Money? Why do you need money?
- So that I can eat.
- I see. And why do you need to eat?
- So that I can work tomorrow, too.

Curious cycle, isn't it? All children are content with what they come into this world. Then, their innate abilities are taken so that they can make money, which they can spend on relearning what they once knew. The only sense I can make of this adventure is that it comes with the experience of learning and growth.

Nonetheless, it saddens me that so many people live in the role of that haggard passenger and do not even attempt

No Excuses!

to get closer to their dreams. This next thought is also from Tony Robbins: "There is only one thing that stands in the way of your getting what you want: The story that you constantly tell yourself!" (I am too old/young/sick, etc.) This story gives you protection: That is why you made it up in the first place. But it also enslaves you. The question is whether you have the courage to break free by realizing this and by working on yourself. You don't have to do it all on your own. Just as I asked for professional help to realize my Ironman goal, you can always reach out for help and support from those who have already achieved your aspirations. This can speed up your progress and spare you a lot of unnecessary pain, as my example shows. If you feel that I'm the right person to accompany you on your journey, get in touch at davidsolyomi.com.

Regardless of what it is that you'd like to spend your days doing, stop for a moment and think about from whom you want to differentiate yourself. From mass amounts of people, who have never even attempted to create something, and are aimlessly drifting. If you are enthusiastic about something, you'll be surprised how quickly you will be recognized! I, for instance, began by taking Brian Tracy's advice, and made sure to read about investing for one hour every day, because that's what I felt drawn to. My economics degree got me nowhere, even though I studied at the country's most reputable university in that field. Thanks to the daily one hour reading sessions, in a few years I was able to go through every piece of literature out there that seemed worth reading, and I put together an approach that made me a successful investor and financially free. (I know that a few years may seem too much, and quicker results sound more attractive. But with that said, it also seems odd to me that those who do not have a few years to spare for something of such importance are perfectly alright working 40 years, numbed by hopelessness.)

Confessions of an Ironman

An hour a day does not take much away from anything, but added up, you become an expert in your chosen field in a few years. When I was sitting over the first book, trying to make sense of what I was reading, I didn't think that there would come a day when I would be corresponding with renowned investors managing billions of dollars, and be treated as an equal partner, presenting arguments of matching calibers. The best investment is to actively seek what you are passionate about; be brave, and show who you are, with the honesty of a child while letting go of the "learned" adult limitations.

If you have true courage, and it is not only pedal cadences and heart rate zones that fascinate you but parts of the book which are about self-discovery, then I'd like to pose one more difficult question for you to ponder: Who are you? If you forget about the learned roles (husband/wife, man/woman, boss/employee, parent, athlete, investor, etc.), when you peel away all of those layers, what is left? One can keep collecting titles – the Ironman is also one, in its own category – but one of the happiest and most liberating days of my life was when I put down my general manager, managing director, and board membership positions, all at once. They would surely look impressive on a business card today, but those are not what make me who I am; I don't identify with titles any longer.

The beauty of learning and (self)discovery is that it's never ending, because otherwise life would be boring, and even those amoebas in that experiment couldn't cope with boredom. When I was a child, my goal to live off of my investments and "retire" young was faulty. The answer does not lie in retirement or complete inactivity. There is an article in the Harvard Business Review[18] on this topic which I highly recommend reading; it's very illuminating. I tried "retirement" for one month, and I drove everyone around me crazy. Lucky for them, I realized that instead of dangling my feet all day, I'd rather pass on what I am good at: Sensible investing. I encourage you to keep searching so that you can also find what motivates you!

---

[18] Why Retirement Is a Flawed Concept (https://hbr.org/2016/04/why-retirement-is-a-flawed-concept).

Gravity Affects You, Even If You Don't Believe in It!

Learning and self-development should never come to an end if you are determined to live a fulfilling life. I first heard from Bodo Schaefer that **success cannot be bought, you can only rent it. And the rental fee is due every day!**

Accept the fact that entropy is part of our world, which basically means that things cannot remain constant: Those who don't progress, regress. Naturally, you do not have to believe in this, but its trueness still remains. It is like gravity: You may deny its existence, but you would still fall from the top of a building.

Entropy is not a bad thing; it simply states that continuous work, learning, and development is the way to go. It is in perfect harmony with the teachings of Tony Robbins: "Progress equals happiness." If each detectable step forward can bring you happiness, why would you not do something every day? This is a frame of mind which I am convinced most successful people have made their own.

I still read about investing because I feel I will be able to learn new things until my very last day. Just like in other areas of life, where I also have quite a bit of room for development. I am never bored, and I like that!

I once read a comment on the internet that said "the Ironman can be fought through without any prior experience or significant preparation." Since I put quite a bit of work into it, this remark made me pause and think for a while. Here is my conclusion: Sure, it may be possible to grind through an Ironman, but you'd only be able to genuinely enjoy it if you consciously prepared for it. I do believe that the journey is truly the goal itself, and while on that journey, make sure to collect everything you can so that you may use that later to further improve your life. I sincerely hope that I was able

Confessions of an Ironman

to show you that this experience can be more than something you just "fight through," it can help you learn from the whole adventure.

Finally, let me share two intriguing WHYs with you, because, in the end, that's what it all comes down to.

This is what John Collins, the founding father of the Ironman, put on the last page of the contest notice of the very first race: "Swim 2.4 miles! Ride 112 miles! Run 26.2 miles! Brag for the rest of your life!"

And if you want more than bragging rights, replace the word *marathon* with *Ironman*, and think about the following lines:

"The marathon shakes you to the core. It deconstructs your very essence, stripping away all of your protective barriers and exposing your inner soul. At a time when you are most vulnerable, the marathon shows no pity."[19]

Happy journey.....in every possible sense of the word!

---

[19] http://www.runnersworld.com/deans-blog/the-marathon

APPENDIX

THE TRAINING PLAN FOR THE 2016 NAGYATÁD RACE

Training hours by weekly breakdown. The horizontal lines separate each training cycle.

week	swim	run	bike	strength training	race	total
1	3.0	2.5	3.0	1.5	0.0	**10.0**
2	3.0	2.8	3.2	1.5	0.0	**10.5**
3	3.0	3.0	3.2	1.5	0.0	**10.7**
4	2.0	2.5	1.8	1.5	0.0	**7.8**
5	3.0	2.8	3.2	1.5	0.0	**10.4**
6	3.0	3.8	3.2	1.0	0.0	**10.9**
7	2.0	2.5	1.8	1.0	0.0	**7.3**
8	3.0	3.2	3.2	1.5	0.0	**10.8**
9	3.0	3.2	3.2	1.5	0.0	**10.8**
10	3.0	3.8	4.0	1.5	0.0	**12.3**
11	3.0	2.5	1.8	1.5	0.0	**8.8**
12	3.0	3.8	4.0	1.5	0.0	**12.3**
13	3.0	3.8	4.0	1.5	0.0	**12.3**
14	3.0	4.1	4.5	1.5	0.0	**13.1**
15	3.0	2.5	1.8	1.5	0.0	**8.8**

Confessions of an Ironman

16	3.0	4.2	5.0	1.5	0.0	**13.7**
17	3.0	4.3	5.0	1.5	0.0	**13.8**
18	3.0	4.4	5.0	1.0	0.0	**13.4**
19	3.0	2.5	1.8	1.5	0.0	**8.8**
20	3.0	4.7	7.5	0.5	0.0	**15.7**
21	3.0	2.2	5.0	1.0	3.6	**14.8** Vienna Marathon
22	3.0	4.3	8.2	1.0	0.0	**16.5**
23	2.0	2.5	1.8	1.5	0.0	**7.8**
24	3.0	4.2	8.5	1.0	0.0	**16.7**
25	3.0	4.2	9.0	1.0	0.0	**17.2**
26	3.0	4.5	4.0	0.5	8.0	**20.0** Ride Around Lake Balaton
27	3.0	2.8	5.5	0.5	0.0	**11.8**
28	3.0	2.5	7.0	1.0	2.8	**16.3** Velence Olympic Distance
29	3.0	5.5	9.8	1.0	0.0	**19.3**
30	3.0	3.8	7.5	1.0	0.0	**15.3**
31	2.0	1.8	4.0	0.5	5.5	**13.8** Kenese Half-distance
32	3.0	5.0	8.3	0.5	0.0	**16.8**
33	3.0	5.0	9.8	1.0	0.0	**18.8**
34	3.0	2.8	5.5	0.5	0.0	**11.8**
35	3.0	6.0	10.8	0.5	0.0	**20.3**
36	3.0	3.8	7.8	0.5	0.0	**15.0**
37	2.0	2.0	2.0	0.0	11.5	**17.5** Nagyatád Full-distance

Appendix

THE TRAINING PLAN FOR THE 2018 IRONMAN BARCELONA

Training hours by weekly breakdown. The horizontal lines separate each training cycle.

week	swim	run	bike	strength training	race	total	
1	3.0	7.0	2.0	0.5	0.0	**12.5**	
2	3.0	7.7	2.0	0.5	0.0	**13.2**	
3	3.0	2.8	2.0	0.5	0.0	**8.3**	
4	3.0	8.0	2.0	0.5	0.0	**13.5**	
5	3.0	6.0	2.0	0.5	0.0	**11.5**	
6	1.0	2.0	1.0	0.0	3.7	**7.7**	Frankfurt Marathon
7	2.0	5.0	2.3	0.0	0.0	**9.3**	
8	3.0	6.5	2.3	0.5	0.0	**12.3**	
9	3.0	4.4	2.3	1.0	0.0	**10.6**	
10	2.0	2.9	1.1	1.0	3.3	**10.3**	Florence Marathon
11	3.0	3.7	2.3	0.0	0.0	**8.9**	
12	3.0	3.8	2.5	1.0	0.0	**10.3**	
13	3.0	3.8	2.7	1.0	0.0	**10.5**	
14	3.0	3.2	2.9	1.0	0.0	**10.1**	
15	2.0	3.6	2.0	0.0	0.0	**7.6**	
16	3.0	5.2	3.2	0.0	0.0	**11.3**	
17	3.0	4.4	3.6	1.0	0.0	**12.0**	
18	3.0	4.8	3.8	1.0	0.0	**12.7**	
19	3.0	3.4	2.0	1.0	0.0	**9.4**	
20	3.0	5.2	4.0	1.0	0.0	**13.2**	
21	3.0	5.3	4.2	1.0	0.0	**13.4**	
22	3.0	5.2	4.3	1.0	0.0	**13.6**	
23	0.0	3.7	2.0	0.0	0.0	**5.7**	

Confessions of an Ironman

24	3.0	5.3	4.5	1.0	0.0	**13.8**	
25	3.0	5.9	4.8	1.0	0.0	**14.7**	
26	3.0	4.0	7.0	1.0	0.0	**15.0**	
27	2.0	1.9	2.0	1.0	0.0	**6.9**	
28	2.0	4.2	7.0	1.0	0.0	**14.2**	
29	3.0	4.0	8.4	0.0	0.0	**15.4**	
30	3.0	2.4	6.1	1.0	0.0	**12.5**	
31	2.0	3.6	8.9	1.0	0.0	**15.6**	
32	3.0	5.1	6.1	1.0	0.0	**15.2**	
33	2.0	2.5	9.4	0.0	0.0	**13.9**	
34	2.0	3.0	5.5	1.0	0.0	**11.5**	
35	3.0	2.1	4.9	1.0	0.0	**11.0**	
36	2.0	1.4	4.0	0.0	5.0	**12.4**	Kenese Half-distance
37	3.0	4.0	8.3	0.0	0.0	**15.3**	
38	2.0	1.2	2.6	1.0	5.5	**12.3**	Keszthely Half-distance
39	3.0	3.3	7.3	1.0	0.0	**14.6**	
40	3.0	4.4	11.0	0.3	0.0	**18.6**	
41	3.0	5.0	11.3	0.3	0.0	**19.6**	
42	2.0	1.7	2.6	0.3	2.4	**9.0**	Szombathely Olympic Distance
43	3.0	4.6	9.7	0.3	0.0	**17.5**	
44	3.0	5.4	10.1	0.3	0.0	**18.8**	
45	1.7	2.2	2.5	0.0	6.0	**12.3**	Nagyatád Relay
46	3.0	4.9	10.9	0.3	0.0	**19.1**	
47	3.0	4.3	10.6	0.3	0.0	**18.3**	
48	2.0	1.8	4.6	0.0	5.1	**13.5**	Tata Half-distance
49	1.0	3.9	8.0	0.0	0.0	**12.9**	
50	2.0	5.3	12.7	0.3	0.0	**20.2**	
51	2.0	5.6	13.4	0.3	0.0	**21.2**	
52	3.0	2.8	6.6	1.0	0.0	**13.3**	
53	2.0	5.1	12.6	0.3	0.0	**19.9**	
54	2.0	4.2	10.6	0.3	0.0	**17.0**	
55	1.8	2.3	4.6	0.0	10.8	**19.5**	Ironman Barcelona

ABOUT THE AUTHOR

Dávid Sólyomi was born in Hungary, in 1982. He graduated as an economist specializing in corporate finance in Budapest and took part in the foundation of both Hungarian and American companies as an entrepreneur. Today, he is living off of the dividends of his investments, and he teaches all over the world how financial freedom can be achieved by purchasing ownership stakes in the world's best companies and receiving a share of their profits in the form of dividends. Neither his acquisition of a solid financial background at a young age, nor his earlier best-selling books made him good enough for himself, so he decided to complete an Ironman triathlon race. This book came to be because that adventure gave him much more than the attractive-sounding title. Dávid has a limited number of one-on-one coaching opportunities available. Please reach out to him at davidsolyomi.com to discuss how he can help you achieve your goals.

I'm reluctant to enter the water (Ironman 70.3 Budapest).

Only at the very end was I so cheerful (Ironman 70.3 Budapest).

The look in my eyes already shows that I will not stop at the half-distance race (Ironman 70.3 Budapest).

So far so good – all the bottles are still in place (eXtremeMan Nagyatád).

It took many years of hard work to earn this finisher shot (eXtremeMan Nagyatád).

It would not have happened without Anikó (Ironman 70.3 Budapest).

The failed execution of the nutrition plan is written all over my face (Ironman Barcelona).

I had just enough left in the tank for a final smile (Ironman Barcelona).